In Other Words

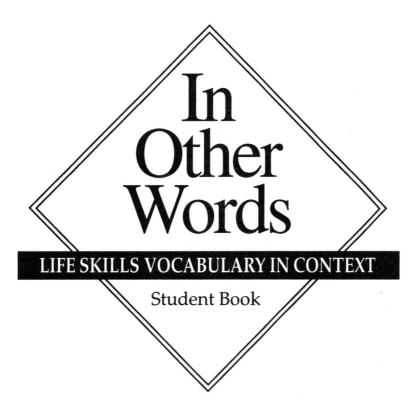

In Other Words

LIFE SKILLS VOCABULARY IN CONTEXT

Student Book

KATHLEEN SANTOPIETRO WEDDEL

Dominie Press, Inc.

Publisher: Raymond Yuen
Executive Editor: Carlos A. Byfield
Editorial Assistant: Bob Rowland
Art Director: Jana C. Whitney
Text Design: Jill Pittsford
Illustrations: Kim Muslusky
Cover Design: Carol Anne Craft

First printing 1989
Reprinted 1990
Reprinted 1991
Reprinted 1992
Reprinted 1994
Revised edition 1998

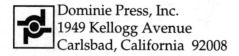
Dominie Press, Inc.
1949 Kellogg Avenue
Carlsbad, California 92008

ISBN 1-56270-019-7
Printed in U.S.A.

6 7 8 9 10 00 99 98

Contents

Acknowledgments

Field test sites and coordinators

Barbara Sample
Director of Educational Services
Spring Institute for International Studies
Wheat Ridge, Colorado

Margaret Silver
Director of Education
International Institute
St. Louis, Missouri

Lucy Stromquist
Area Resource Teacher
St. Vrain Valley Schools
Longmont, Colorado

Reviewers and technical assistance

Virginia French Allen
Academic Consultant
Spring Institute for International Studies
Wheat Ridge, Colorado

Dian Bates
State Director
Adult Basic Education
Denver, Colorado

Mark A. Clarke
Associate Professor and Chair
Language, Literacy, and Culture
School of Education
University of Colorado at Denver
Denver, Colorado

The author wishes to thank Ruth and Elvin Graves for their words of support and encouragement. Inspiration for this book belongs to Leonard and our Saratoga friends.

Introduction

In Other Words: Life Skills Vocabulary in Context provides meaningful activities that reinforce and enhance the vocabulary used in survival English settings. While a core life skills text may provide vocabulary through dialogue, grammar lessons, or pronunciation exercises, students may need further vocabulary practice. The material in this book has been designed to accompany and complement instruction in a life skills curriculum.

Each of the 10 units identifies vocabulary of life skills topics that are common in adult ESL classrooms: personal information, health, housing, American government, shopping for food and clothing, transportation, community services, money and banking, and employment.

Each unit contains the following features:

- "Picture It" — Illustrations at the beginning of the unit. Provides meaning for the vocabulary used in the exercises that follow.

- "Give It a Try" — Word substitution exercise. Provides practice of words in context.

- "Attention, Please" — Multiple choice exercise. Provides practice in listening and reading skills.

- "Tell Me About It" — Pair activity. One student has information that another student doesn't have, but needs, to complete a task.

- "Guess Who, Where, or What" — Category activity. Checks student's understanding of word meanings.

- "Two Against One" — Category exercise. Makes use of reading and speaking skills. Checks student's understanding of word meaning and usage.

- "Inside Story" — Fill in the blank exercise. Facilitates student's use of contextual clues. Provides practice in finding synonyms.

- "Take Your Pick" — Multiple choice exercise. Checks student's understanding of sentence meaning and vocabulary usage.

- "Bingo" — Bingo game. Provides a spelling assessment as well as listening practice.

- "Get It Together" — Crossword puzzle. Provides practice in recognizing word meaning and usage.

Unit
1

PERSONAL INFORMATION

Picture It

The following pictures show people and things that will be discussed in this unit. Refer to these pictures when doing exercises throughout the unit.

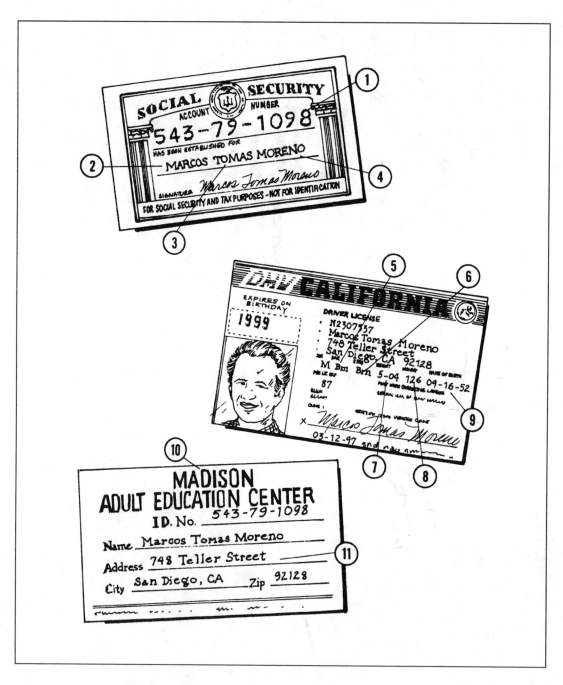

1. _____
2. _____
3. _____
4. _____
5. _____
6. _____
7. _____
8. _____
9. _____
10. _____
11. _____

1._____

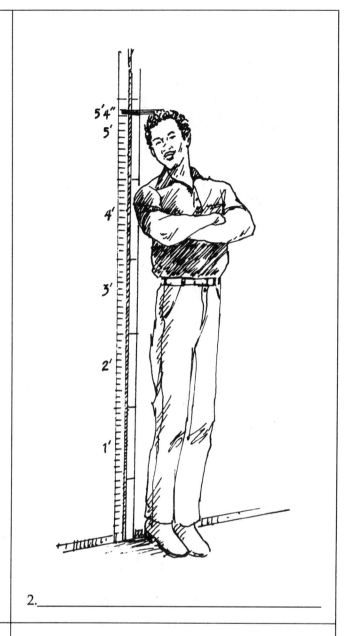

2._____

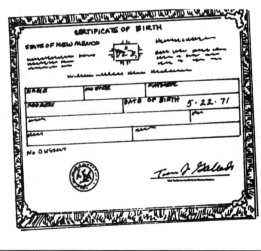

3._____

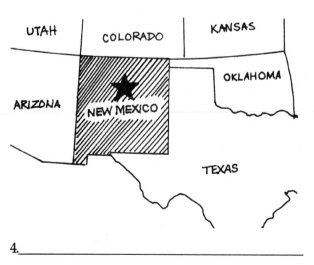

4._____

5._____

6._____

7._____

8._____

9._____

10._____

11._____

12._____

MARCOS TOMAS MORENO

13._____

MARCOS TOMAS MORENO

14._____

MARCOS TOMAS MORENO

15._____

16._____

17._____

18._____

19._____

20._____

Give It a Try

Follow the teacher's instructions to practice the phrases below.

1. Write your <u>last name</u> here.
   > first name
   > middle name
   > height

2. What's your <u>birth date</u>? <u>May 15, 1969</u>
   > birthplace   San Salvador
   > ZIP Code   90056
   > area code   213

3. What <u>city</u> does he live in? <u>Austin</u>
   > apartment   number 308
   > state   Texas

4. She lives alone, she is <u>single</u>.
   > divorced
   > separated
   > widowed

5. He has been <u>married</u> for eight years.
   > divorced
   > employed
   > unemployed

6. What's your <u>work</u> address? <u>1986 Fell Street</u>.
   > home   1355 56th Street
   > school   1219 Grand Avenue

7. Write your <u>telephone</u> number here.
   > Social Security
   > work
   > apartment

8. <u>Marcos</u> circled <u>male</u> on the application.
   > Marta   female
   > Ray   Mr.
   > Tury   Mrs.

Attention, Please!

Listen to the teacher's cue. Then, circle the correct response.

1. birth date   birthplace   city

2. ZIP Code   area code   address

3. apartment   phone number   address

4. birth date   birthplace   height

5. height   ZIP Code   weight

6. Social Security Number   mailing address   home address

7. married   single   widowed

8. first name   last name   middle name

9. height   weight   married

10. ZIP Code   phone number   area code

11. 145 pounds   5' 7"   89076

12. 9/4/50   135 pounds   432-0987

Tell Me About It (Part A)

Study the application form. Then, ask your partner the questions below. Fill in the form with your partner's answers.

What's the person's last name?
What's his street address?
What's his phone number?
What's his birth date?
How tall is he?

How old is he?
What's the date?
What state does he live in?
What city does he live in?

Name _____ Sam _____ Luis _____
       LAST   FIRST   MIDDLE

Address _____ #42
              STREET   APT. NO.

_____ 80221
       CITY   STATE   ZIP CODE

Telephone Number (303) _____
                   AREA CODE

Height _____ Weight __145 lbs.__ Age _____

Birth Date _____ Birthplace __México__
           MO. / DAY / YR.

[ ] Married [X] Single [ ] Divorced [ ] Separated [ ] Widowed

[X] Employed [ ] Unemployed

Place of Employment __Smith Machine Shop__

Signature __Sam L. Lopez__ Date _____

Tell Me About It (Part B)

Study the application form. Then, ask your partner the questions below. Fill in the form with your partner's answers.

What's the person's first name?

What's his middle name?

What's the apartment number?

What's the area code?

What's the ZIP Code?

How much does he weigh?

Is he married?

Where was he born?

Where is he working?

Name _____ Lopez _____

           LAST   FIRST   MIDDLE

Address _____ 526 Blue Street _____

                 STREET   APT. NO.

_____ Denver _____ Colorado _____

             CITY   STATE   ZIP CODE

Telephone Number (_____) 778-4120 _____

                     AREA CODE

Height _____ Weight _____ Age ___ 36 ___

Birth Date ___ 6/15/62 _____ Birthplace _____

                   MO. / DAY / YR.

☐ Married   ☐ Single   ☐ Divorced   ☐ Separated   ☐ Widowed

☐ Employed   ☐ Unemployed

Place of Employment _____

Signature ___ *Sam L. Lopez* _____ Date ___ April 14, 1999 ___

Guess Who, Where, or What

Read each word or phrase in the list below. Ask a classmate if the word or phrase describes a person, place, or thing. Write the words in the correct category.

married	single	ZIP Code
addresss	area code	phone number
Social Security Number	divorced	weight
widowed	age	middle name
first name	state	city
birth date	birthplace	height
last name	male	female
employed	unemployed	place of employment

Words That Describe Us	Information Places	Information Numbers

Two Against One

Circle the word that doesn't belong to the set. Explain your choice.

1. first name   last name   address

2. divorced   married   separated

3. ZIP Code   area code   phone number

4. city   female   state

5. state   male   female

6. employed   unemployed   place of employment

7. married   single   divorced

8. height   weight   face

9. last name   ZIP Code   signature

10. age   birthplace   birth date

11. 120 pounds   weight   height

12. height   5'8"   ZIP Code

Inside Story

Read the story below. Choose words or phrases from the list that have the same meanings as the words or phrases under the lines. Write the correct words on the blanks. Read the story again using the words written on the blanks.

middle name	picture	glad
renew	weight	height
identification	address	city
last name	answer	test
age	birth date	

Juanita's Driver's License

Juanita went to _____ her driver's license. She passed the written
                  (replace)

_____ . She passed the driving test. Then, she had to
    (exam)

_____ some questions.
  (respond to)

The clerk asked for the spelling of her_____ . Juanita spelled her
                             (family name)

_____ too. She gave her new _____ . She lives
  (second name)   (house number)

in the same _____ but moved to a new apartment last month.
        (town)

The officer asked Juanita for her _____ and
                    (how tall she is)

_____ and her eye and hair color. He also needed to know her
(how much she weighs)

_____ and _____ . After the questions, the
  (day of birth)   (how old she is)

officer took Juanita's _____ for _____ . Juanita
            (photo)   (I.D.)

smiled. She was _____ it was over.
        (happy)

Take Your Pick

There is a missing word or phrase in each sentence below. Read each sentence. Then, look at the three choices under the sentence. Choose the correct word or phrase and write it on the blank.

1. He circled the word _____ on his application form.

   female   male   sex

2. Fidel lives in the _____ of California.

   area code   address   state

3. Tom's _____ is May 26, 1948.

   birthplace   birth date   city

4. Lupe gave her _____ as 5 feet, 2 inches.

   height   weight   hair color

5. Write your _____ first.

   name last   first   last name

6. Binh gave his _____ as 135 pounds.

   weight   height   phone number

7. What's your _____?

   Social Number Security   Social Security Number   Security Social Number

8. _____ at the bottom, please.

   Signs   Signing   Sign

9. Maria has been _____ for 12 years.

   married   marriage   marry

10. Write the _____ before the phone number.

    ZIP Code   city   area code

Bingo

1. Make your bingo card.
Your teacher reads a word or phrase. Choose any square and write the word or phrase inside that square. Write one word or phrase in each square. Don't fill in the squares in order.

2. Check your spelling.
The teacher writes the words on the board. Find the correct spelling of each word and check your card. Correct any mistakes.

3. Play bingo.
The teacher reads a clue. Find the square containing the word or phrase that has the same meaning as the teacher's clue. Cover the square with a marker. When you have three covered squares in a row, you have BINGO!

Get It Together

There is a word missing in each sentence below. Choose the correct word from the word list. Print that word in the boxes of the puzzle.

city	Code	height
information	name	first
married	single	birth
address	age	Social

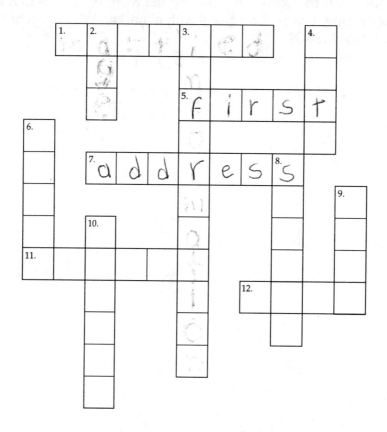

Across

1. She was _____ to Emilio for 12 years.

5. Her _____ name is Mary.

7. His _____ is 509 Reed Place.

11. His _____ is 6 feet, 2 inches.

12. What's your last _____ ?

Down

2. She gave her _____ as 45 years.

3. They ask for personal _____ .

4. Every _____ has a different ZIP Code.

6. His _____ date is 4/12/52.

8. What's your _____ Security number?

9. What's your ZIP _____ ?

10. She's not married; she's _____ .

Unit 2

HEALTH

Picture It

The following pictures show people and things that will be discussed in this unit. Refer to these pictures when doing exercises throughout the unit.

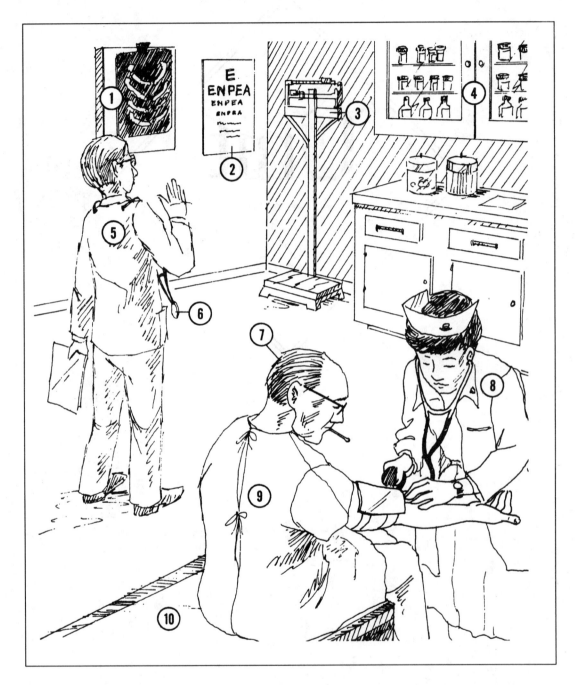

1._____   5._____   9._____

2._____   6._____   10._____

3._____   7._____

4._____   8._____

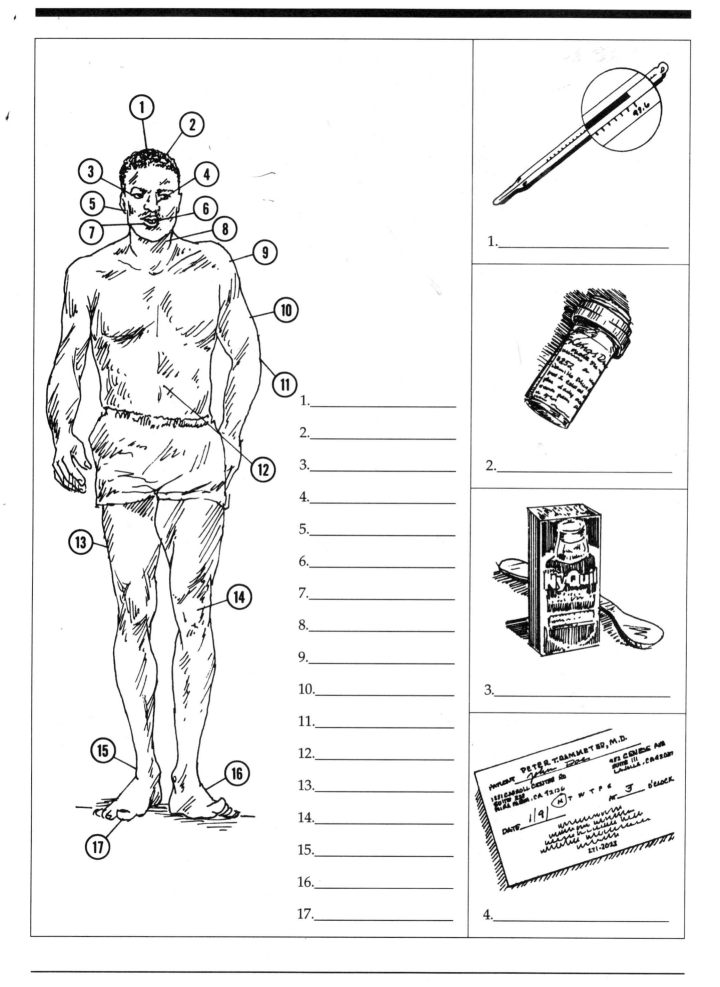

1._____

2._____

3._____

4._____

5._____

6._____

7._____

8._____

9._____

10._____

11._____

12._____

13._____

14._____

15._____

16._____

17._____

1._____

2._____

3._____

4._____

5._____

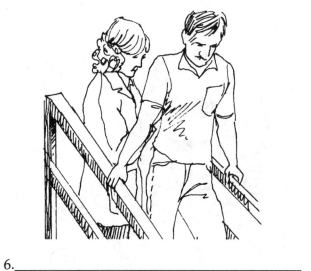

6._____

7._____

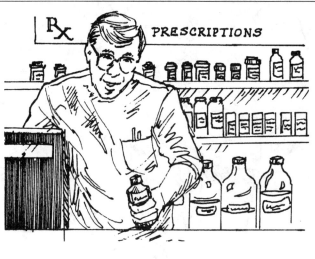

8._____

9._____

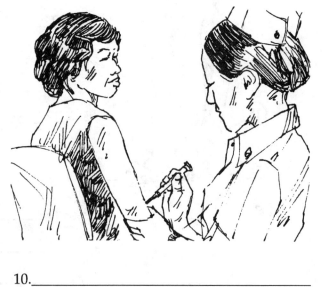

10._____

11._____

12._____

13._____

14._____

15._____

16._____

17._____

18._____

19._____

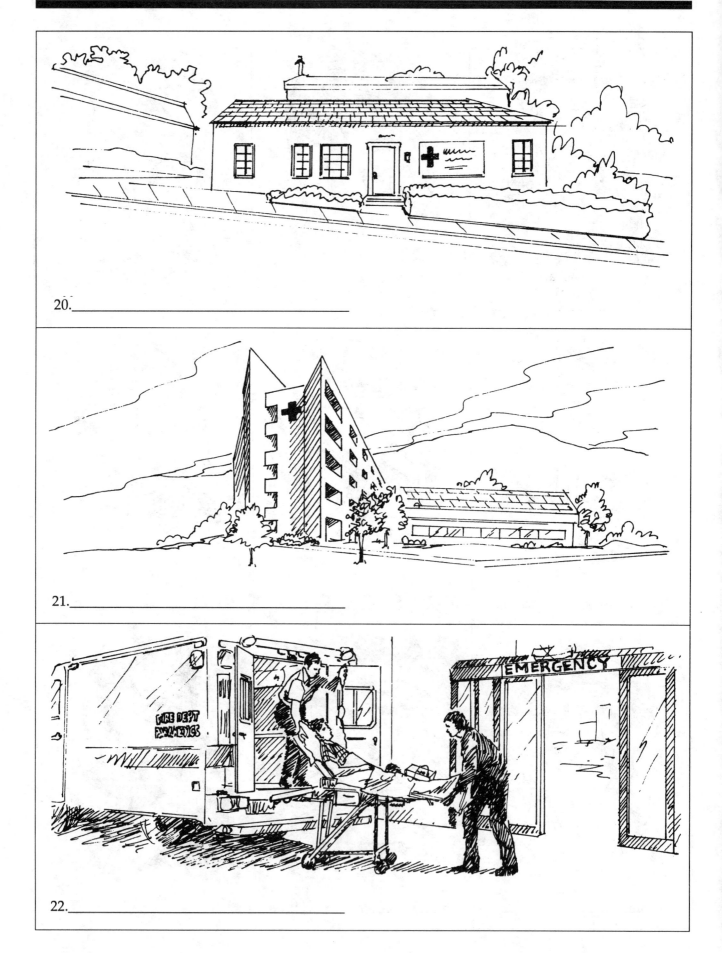

20._____

21._____

22._____

Give It a Try

Follow the teacher's instructions to practice the phrases below.

1. Did they check your _blood pressure_ at the clinic? _Yes, they did_ .

    temperature
    pulse
    heartbeat   No, they didn't.
    X-rays

2. My son has a _headache_ . He should _buy some aspirin_ .

    backache   get some rest
    toothache   see the dentist
    sore throat   see the doctor

3. Where is the ___hospital___ ? It's ___across the street___ .

    clinic   two blocks away
    pharmacy   straight down the hall
    emergency room   on the first floor

4. My _chest_ hurts. My _shoulders_ hurt.

    leg   feet
    arm   eyes
    ankle   fingers
    foot   hands

5. The ___doctor___ is at the ___clinic___ .

    surgeon   hospital
    therapist   office
    pharmacist   drugstore

6. You may buy ___some aspirin___ at the drugstore.

    some cough syrup
    a thermometer
    some medicine

7. The _doctor_ uses a ___stethoscope___ in an exam.

    nurse   thermometer
                 blood pressure cuff
                 scale

Attention, Please!

Listen to the teacher's cue. Then, circle the correct response.

1. patient   surgeon   pharmacist

2. patient   surgeon   therapist

3. nurse   doctor   pharmacist

4. nurse   doctor   pharmacist

5. therapist   ambulance driver   receptionist

6. nurse   receptionist   patient

7. blood pressure cuff   thermometer   stethoscope

8. stethoscope   blood sample   thermometer

9. prescription medicine   nonprescription medicine   pharmacy

10. eye chart   surgeon   scale

11. broken arm   shoulders   fever

12. clinic   hospital   X-ray lab

Tell Me About It (Part A)

Study the picture. Then, ask your partner the questions below. Using your partner's answers, write the name of each underlined item in the correct place on the grid.

Where's the <u>examining table</u>?   Where's the <u>thermometer</u>?
Where's the <u>stethoscope</u>?   Where's the <u>scale</u>?
Where's the <u>doctor</u>?

1.	2.	3.
4.	5.	6.
7.	8.	9.

Tell Me About It (Part B)

Study the picture. Then, ask your partner the questions below. Using your partner's answers, write the name of each underlined item in the correct place on the grid.

Where's the <u>X-ray</u>?   Where's the <u>blood pressure cuff</u>?
Where's the <u>eye chart</u>?   Where's the <u>nurse</u>?

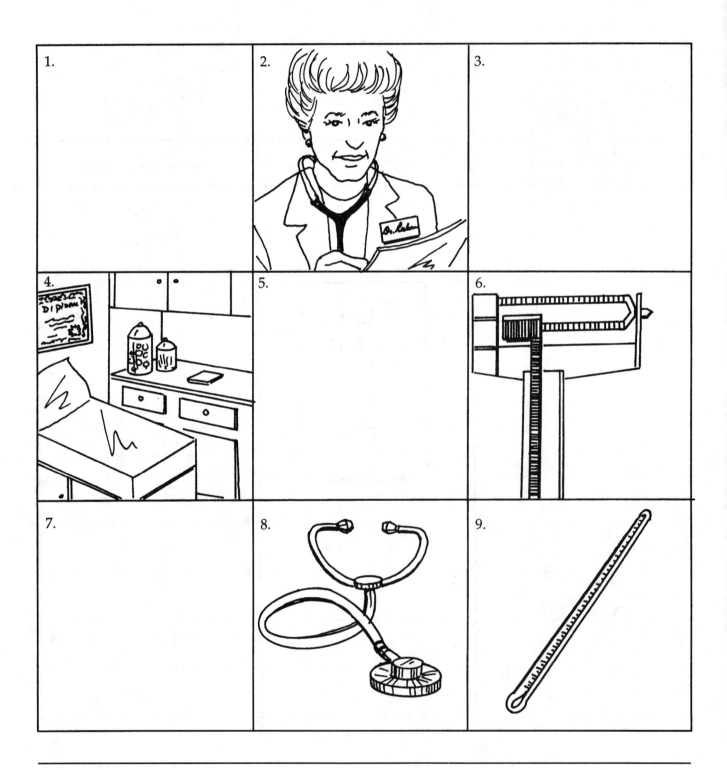

Guess Who, Where, or What

Read each word or phrase in the list below. Ask a classmate if the word or phrase describes a person, place, or thing. Write the words in the correct category.

doctor
blood pressure cuff
hospital
gown
ambulance driver
pharmacist
examining room
emergency room

nurse
clinic
eye chart
blood sample
surgeon
stethoscope
receptionist

therapist
thermometer
examining table
X-ray lab
pharmacy
X-ray
scale

Health Workers	Places for Health Services	Things a Doctor Uses

Two Against One

Circle the word that doesn't belong to the set. Explain your choice.

1. headache   back   backache

2. nose   mouth   shoulder

3. emergency   hospital   pharmacy

4. ankle   waist   stomach

5. pain   hospital   ache

6. feet   ankle   arm

7. temperature   nurse   thermometer

8. patient   doctor   nurse

9. face   eyes   ears

10. appointment   emergency   clinic

11. stethoscope   X-ray lab   thermometer

12. prescription   aspirin   nonprescription

Inside Story

Read the story below. Choose words or phrases from the list that have the same meanings as the words or phrases under the lines. Write the correct words on the blanks. Read the story again using the words written on the blanks.

doctor	clinic	sick
8	got up	thermometer
3:00 P.M.	fever	receptionist
sore throat	stay in bed	100°
headache	an appointment	temperature

Manuel Is Sick

Manuel is _____ years old. Today he
                    (eight)

_____ late. He was _____ . He had a
  (got out of bed)   (not well)

_____ . He had a _____ . He had a cough. His
  (pain in his throat)   (pain in his head)

mother, Juanita, told him to _____ . Juanita got the
                                (not get up)

_____ to take her son's _____ . It was over
  (thing that tells temperature)   (measure of heat)

_____ ! Manuel had a _____ .
  (one hundred degrees)   (high temperature)

Juanita called the _____ to make _____ for
                      (place for health care)   (a visit time)

Manuel. The _____ said Manuel could see the
                (person answering)

_____ at _____ .
  (Dr.)   (three o'clock in the afternoon)

Take Your Pick

There is a missing word or phrase in each sentence below. Read each sentence. Then, look at the three choices under the sentence. Choose the correct word or phrase and write it on the blank.

1. The nurse took his _____ .

   temperature   thermometer   fever

2. Maria called the clinic to make an early _____ .

   appointment   check-up   examination

3. Tuyet needed a _____ for her new job.

   check-out   checkup   check-around

4. Her _____ was filled at the Baker Pharmacy on 7th Street.

   medicine   appointment   prescription

5. Take a deep _____ .

   breathe   breath   breathing

6. The boy has a _____ leg.

   broken   break   broke

7. Juanita took _____ for her headache.

   aspirin   surgery   checkup

8. Kim has to have _____ on Tuesday morning.

   surgeon   broken arm   surgery

9. The _____ gave me the medicine.

   pharmacist   pharmacy   prescription

10. The nurse took his _____ .

    blood press   pressure blood   blood pressure

Bingo

1. Make your bingo card.
Your teacher reads a word or phrase. Choose any square and write the word or phrase inside that square. Write one word or phrase in each square. Don't fill in the squares in order.

2. Check your spelling.
The teacher writes the words on the board. Find the correct spelling of each word and check your card. Correct any mistakes.

3. Play bingo.
The teacher reads a clue. Find the square containing the word or phrase that has the same meaning as the teacher's clue. Cover the square with a marker. When you have three covered squares in a row, you have BINGO!

Get It Together

There is a word missing in each sentence below. Choose the correct word from the word list. Print that word in the boxes of the puzzle.

doctor   surgeons   eye

receptionist   fever   thermometer

patient   volunteer   nurse

toes   sore   ear

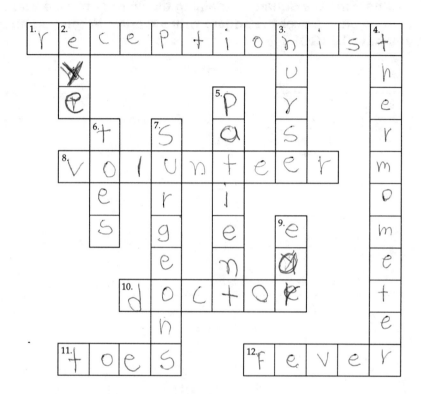

Across

1. The _____ sits at the information desk.

8. A _____ isn't paid.

10. A physician is a _____ .

11. There are 10 _____ on two feet.

12. 101° is a _____ .

Down

2. He closed his left _____ .

3. The _____ took his blood pressure.

4. Use a _____ to take your temperature.

5. The _____ is very sick.

6. I have a _____ throat.

7. Two _____ operated on him.

9. He has wax in his _____ .

Unit
3

HOUSING

Picture It

The following pictures show people and things that will be discussed in this unit. Refer to these pictures when doing exercises throughout the unit.

1._____   4._____   7._____

2._____   5._____

3._____   6._____

1._____   4._____   7._____

2._____   5._____

3._____   6._____

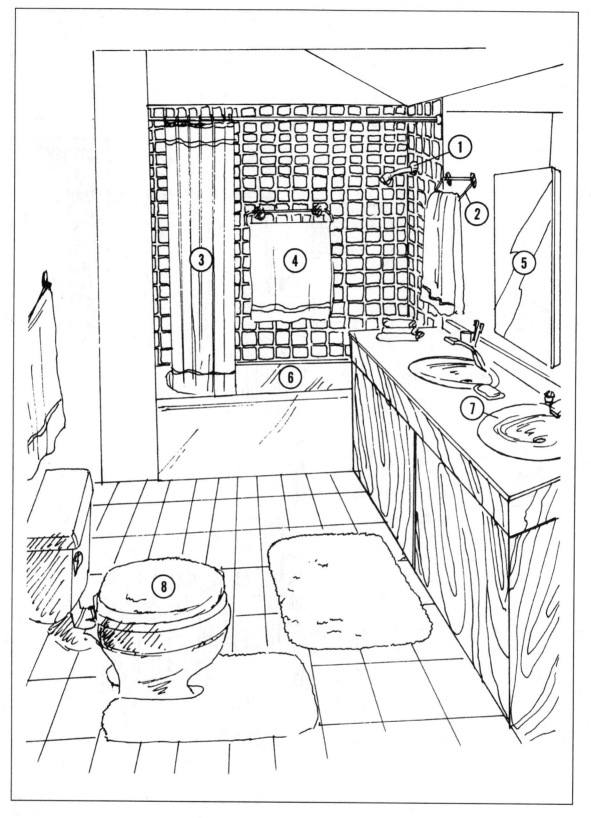

1._____   4._____   7._____

2._____   5._____   8._____

3._____   6._____

1._____ 4._____ 7._____

2._____ 5._____

3._____ 6._____

1._____ 3._____ 5._____

2._____ 4._____ 6._____

1._____ 3._____ 5._____

2._____ 4._____

1._____

2._____

3._____

4._____

5. _____

6. _____

7. _____

8. _____

9._____

10._____

11._____

12._____

Give It a Try

Follow the teacher's instructions to practice the phrases below.

1. _Oscar_ rents _an apartment_.

   Carmen   a house
   Susan   a mobile home
   Ben   a townhouse
   Anita   a duplex

2. The tenant called the _landlord_ for help. What did the _landlord_ say?

   manager   manager
   carpenter   carpenter
   electrician   electrician
   plumber   plumber

3. Please _paint_ the _bedroom_ .

   clean   bathroom
   sweep   basement
   vacuum   living room

4. We need _a rug_ for the _kitchen_ .

   a lamp   bedroom
   towels   bathroom
   chairs   living room

5. The _toilet_ is leaking.

   sink
   bathtub
   shower

6. Does your apartment have a _yard_ ? No, it doesn't.

   garage
   patio
   porch

7. The _____door_____ is broken.

   window
   hot water heater
   cabinet

Attention, Please!

Listen to the teacher's cue. Then, circle the correct response.

1. blinds
    blains

    carpet

    ceiling

2. refrigerator
    refrilleiror

    sofa

    shower

3. picture

    chair
    cher

    curtains
    curens

4. toilet

    cunapara bebe
    crib
    crip

    bed

5. dresser

    sofa

    cabinets
    cavinets

6. towel
    taoo

    lamp

    ceiling

7. toilets

    chairs

    curtains

8. stoves
    estous

    shelves
    cheols

    tables

9. basement
    beisment

    attic

    garage

10. shower

    picture

    floor

11. closet

    stove

    sink

12. refrigerator

    end table

    sink

Tell Me About It (Part A)

Study the picture. Then, ask your partner the questions below. Using your partner's answers, write the name of each underlined item in the correct place on the picture.

Where's the <u>closet</u>?

Where's the <u>refrigerator</u>?

Where's the <u>shower</u>?

Where are the <u>chairs</u>?

Where's the <u>hot water heater</u>?

Where's the <u>dining room table</u>?

Where's the <u>bookshelf</u>?

Where's the <u>window</u> (upstairs)?

Where's the <u>window</u> (downstairs)?

Is there a <u>car</u> in the garage?

Is there a <u>bed</u> in the bedroom?

Is there a <u>bathtub</u> in the bathroom?

Are there <u>cabinets</u> in the kitchen?

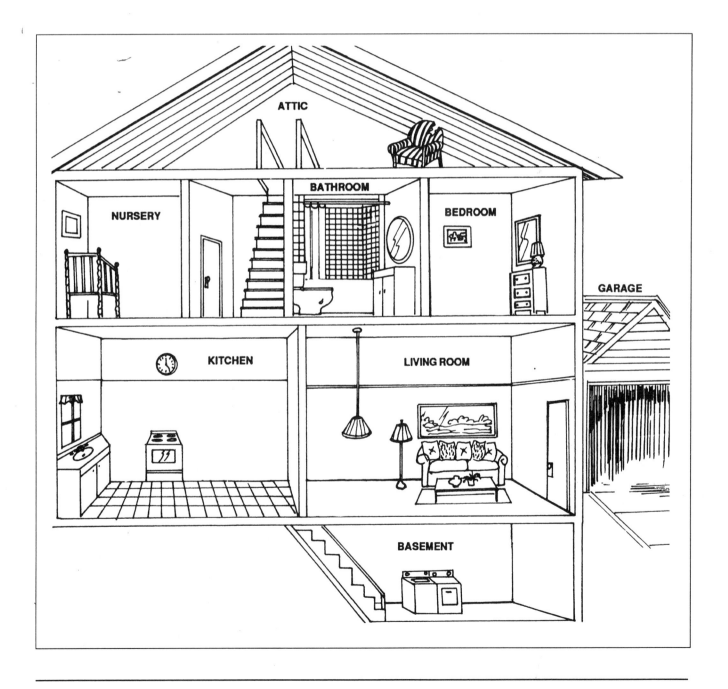

Tell Me About It (Part B)

Study the picture. Then, ask your partner the questions below. Using your partner's answers, write the name of each underlined item in the correct place on the picture.

Where's the <u>dresser</u>?

Where's the <u>lamp</u>?

Where's the <u>dryer</u>?

Where's the <u>sink</u>?

Where's the <u>sofa</u>?

Where's the <u>floor lamp</u>?

Where's the <u>toilet</u>?

Where did they put the <u>crib</u>?

Where did they put the <u>clock</u>?

Where did they put the <u>picture</u>?

Where did they put the <u>stove</u>?

Where's the <u>old chair</u>?

Where's the <u>washer</u>?

Guess Who, Where, or What

Read each word or phrase in the list below. Ask a classmate if the word or phrase describes a person, place, or thing. Write the words in the correct category.

landlord	kitchen	walls
patio	screen door	dining room
super	plumber	cabinets
window	carpenter	floor
real estate agent	electrician	corner
manager	bathroom	living room
bedroom	basement	attic
garage	ceiling	hall
closet	porch	

People Who Work in Housing	Places in a House	Parts of a Room

Two Against One

Circle the word that doesn't belong to the set. Explain your choice.

1. sofa   end table   coffee table

2. refrigerator   sofa   stove

3. toilet   sink   coffee table

4. stove   bed   dresser

5. cabinet   bed   closet

6. tenant   plumber   electrician

7. drapes   duplex   house

8. door   closet   window

9. walls   kitchen   ceiling

10. dining room   mobile home   apartment

11. clock   basement   attic

12. lawn furniture   crib   patio

Inside Story

Read the story below. Choose words or phrases from the list that have the same meanings as the words or phrases under the lines. Write the correct words on the blanks. Read the story again using the words written on the blanks.

deposit	Street	many	rent
walls	leaking	refrigerator	cabinets
excited	manager	an apartment	broken
kitchen	door	bedroom	carpet
ads	shower	very much	

Margaret's Decision

Margaret wanted to rent _____ . She looked at the

(small housing)

_____ in the Sunday newspaper. There were _____

(advertisements)   (a lot of)

apartments!

Margaret went to the apartment on 6th _____ . She asked the

(road)

_____ to show her the apartment. She was _____

(supervisor)   (happy)

until the _____ opened. The _____ was small. The

(entrance)   (cooking place)

_____ were dirty and there was no _____ . The

(cupboards)   (ice box)

_____ window was _____ . The

(sleeping place)   (cracked)

_____ was _____ . The

(bathing place)   (dripping)

_____ needed paint and the _____ was dirty.

(room sides)   (rug)

The manager said the _____ was only $375.00 and the

(money paid each month)

_____ was only $200.00. Margaret said, "Thank you

(dollars paid before)

_____ , but I need to look around."

(a lot)

Take Your Pick

There is a missing word or phrase in each sentence below. Read each sentence. Then, look at the three choices under the sentence. Choose the correct word or phrase and write it on the blank.

1. The _____ is too high.

   rental   renting   rent

2. The _____ came to fix the bathroom sink.

   electrician   plumber   carpenter

3. Juana needs a(n)_____ to put new cabinets in the kitchen.

   electrician   plumber   carpenter

4. Why don't you ask the _____ ?

   electric   electrician   electricity

5. The _____ is cracked.

   wall   carpet   curtains

6. Sarah needs help. The toilet is _____ .

   leaking   leak   leaked

7. The closet _____ is broken.

   drawer   table   door

8. Juana looked up and saw that the _____ was cracked.

   floor   ceiling   rug

9. She had to pay rent and a _____ on the first of the month.

   apartment   damage deposit   lease

10. It was a beautiful summer day, so they decided to eat on the _____.

   kitchen   patio   basement

Bingo

1. Make your bingo card.
Your teacher reads a word or phrase. Choose any square and write the word or phrase inside that square. Write one word or phrase in each square. Don't fill in the squares in order.

2. Check your spelling.
The teacher writes the words on the board. Find the correct spelling of each word and check your card. Correct any mistakes.

3. Play bingo.
The teacher reads a clue. Find the square containing the word or phrase that has the same meaning as the teacher's clue. Cover the square with a marker. When you have three covered squares in a row, you have BINGO!

Get It Together

There is a word missing in each sentence below. Choose the correct word from the word list. Print that word in the boxes of the puzzle.

attic	living room	bathroom
manager	corner	tenant
door	yard	garage
rug	rent	kitchen

Across

3. He's in the _____, resting on the sofa.

6. Pay the _____ on the first of the month.

7. The toilet in the _____ upstairs is broken.

9. The new _____ is on the floor in the bedroom.

10. The _____ pays the rent.

11. She plants flowers in the _____ .

12. The car is in the _____ .

Down

1. He's in the _____, making lunch.

2. The _____ is locked.

4. The _____ collects the rent.

5. Put the table in the _____ of the room.

8. The _____ is the top floor of a house.

Unit 4

Picture It

The following pictures show people and things that will be discussed in this unit. Refer to these pictures when doing exercises throughout the unit.

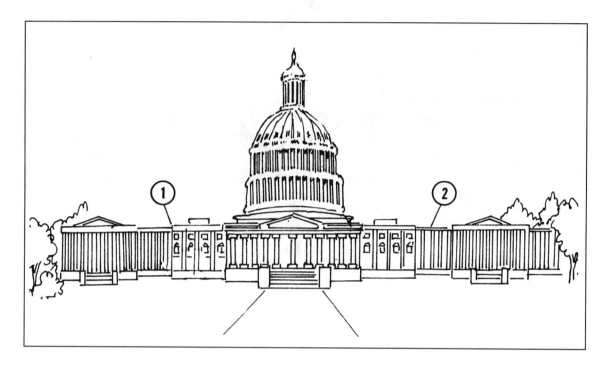

1._____ 2._____

1._____ 2._____

1._____

2._____

3._____

4._____

5._____

6._____

7._____

8._____

9._____

10._____

11._____

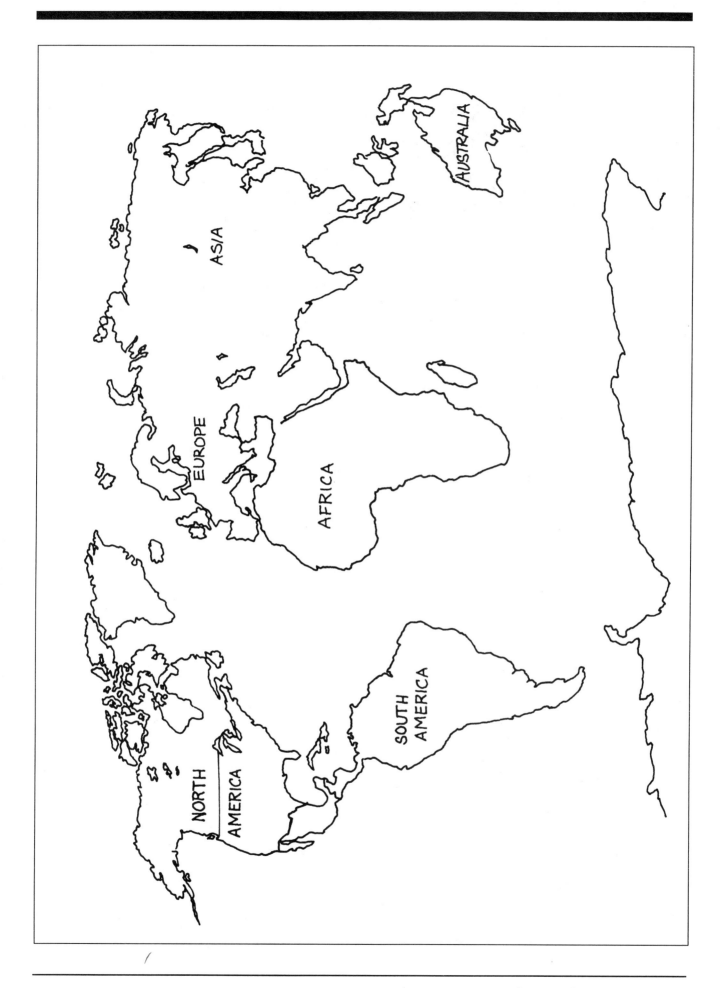

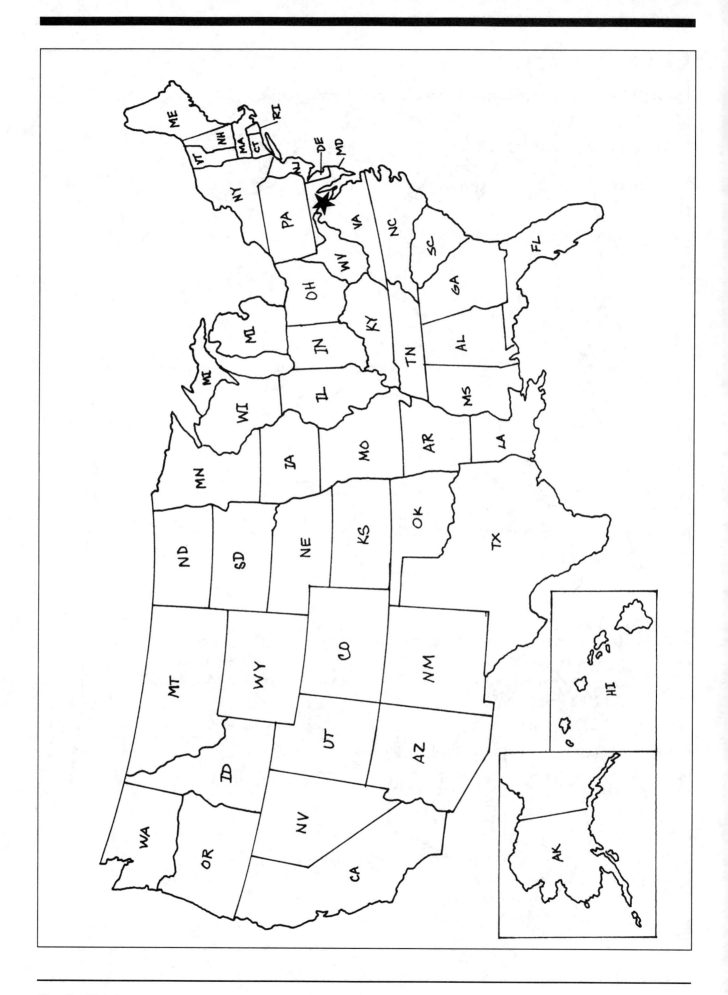

Give It a Try

Follow the teacher's instructions to practice the phrases below.

1. The _eagle_ is a symbol of ___the country___ .

       flag   the nation
       anthem   the United States

2. The people of the _nation_ are the voters.

           state
           city
           U.S.

3. How many _stars_ does the flag have? It has _50_ .

         stripes   13
         colors   3

4. The flag is sometimes called _____Old Glory_____ .

                 the Stars and Stripes
                 the Star Spangled Banner

5. Who _is_ the ___vice-president___ of the United States?

               president
      are   Supreme Court judges
               senators

6. We heard the __president's speech__ on the radio. _Who_ is the _____president_____?

         national anthem   What   national anthem
         Star Spangled Banner   What   Star Spangled Banner
         senator's speech   Who   senator

7. The ___senator___ works in the _legislative_ branch.

       representative   legislative
       president   executive
       judge   judicial

8. Where is the _____White House_____? It's in Washington, D.C.

         Congress
         Supreme Court building
         Capitol building

Attention, Please!

Listen to the teacher's cue. Then, circle the correct response.

1. city   nation   state

2. America   Washington, D.C.   United States

3. red, orange, blue   stars and stripes   red, white, blue

4. legislative branch   executive branch   judicial branch

5. legislative branch   executive branch   judicial branch

6. Senate   government   White House

7. legislative branch   executive branch   judicial branch

8. branch   eagle   nation

9. Star Spangled Banner   the flag   the eagle

10. 13   50   15

11. 13   6   7

12. Old Glory   eagle   national anthem

Tell Me About It (Part A)

Study the picture. Then, ask your partner the questions below. Using your partner's answers, write the name of each underlined item in the correct place on the grid.

Where's the <u>judge</u>?   Where's the <u>supreme court</u>?

Where does the <u>senator</u> work?   Where's the <u>national song</u>?

Where's the <u>flag</u>?

1.	2.	3.
4.	5.	6.
7.	8.	9.

Tell Me About It (Part B)

Study the picture. Then, ask your partner the questions below. Using your partner's answers, write the name of each underlined item in the correct place on the grid.

Where's the <u>eagle</u>?

Where does the <u>representative</u> work?

Where does the <u>president</u> live?

Where's the U.S. <u>map</u>?

1.	2.	3.
4.	5.	6.
7.	8.	9.

Guess Who, Where, or What

Read each word or phrase in the list below. Ask a classmate if the word or phrase describes a person, place, or thing. Write the words in the correct category.

senator   White House   Congress
Washington, D.C.   president   judge
flag   House of Representatives   stars
Star Spangled Banner   Senate   Supreme Court
state capital   representative   eagle
voter   national anthem   national capital
banner   stripes   colors
vice-president

People in Government	Places in Government	Symbols of the Country

Two Against One

Circle the word that doesn't belong to the set. Explain your choice.

1. senator   representative   Senate

2. state capital   Washington, D.C.   national capital

3. red   star   blue

4. America   United States   state

5. country   nation   city

6. branch   flag   eagle

7. judge   senator   Supreme Court

8. president   executive branch   senator

9. legislative branch   executive branch   Congress

10. senator   legislative branch   judge

11. national anthem   Star Spangled Banner   Congress

12. city   America   country

Inside Story

Read the story below. Choose words or phrases from the list that have the same meanings as the words or phrases under the lines. Write the correct words on the blanks. Read the story again using the words written on the blanks.

original	country	number
sometimes	anthem	3
the U.S.	national	flag
represent	coins	stripes
6	50	Spangled
symbol		

Symbols of America

The American _____ is a symbol of our
                              (banner)

_____ . The flag has _____ colors. The colors
                (nation)   (three)

are red, white, and blue. There are _____ stars on the flag. The stars
                                              (fifty)

_____ the _____ of states in
          (stand for)   (no.)

_____ . There are seven red _____ and
          (America)   (lines)

_____ white stripes. The stripes represent the 13
          (six)

_____ states. The flag is _____ called Old
          (first)   (often)

Glory or the Stars and Stripes.

The national _____ was written by Francis Scott Key in 1814. The
                        (song)

national anthem is called the "Star _____ Banner." People sing this song at
                                              (spotted)

_____ celebrations and at the beginning of sports events.
          (countrywide)

The bald eagle is another _____ of America. The eagle is printed on
                                    (sign)

_____ and bills.
          (change)

Take Your Pick

There is a missing word or phrase in each sentence below. Read each sentence. Then, look at the three choices under the sentence. Choose the correct word or phrase and write it on the blank.

1. There are three branches of _____ government.

   Americans   American   America

2. The _____ anthem is the "Star Spangled Banner."

   national   nation   country

3. What are the three branches of _____ ?

   governor   govern   government

4. _____ make laws in congress.

   Senate   Senators   Senator

5. Congress has two houses, the Senate and the House of _____ .

   representative   represent   Representatives

6. The _____ branch makes the laws.

   legislative   legislature   legislate

7. The _____ branch enforces the law.

   executives   judicial   executive

8. The Supreme Court is in the _____ branch.

   judge   judicial   judging

9. There are _____ stars on the flag.

   15   13   50

10. The president lives in the _____ in Washington, D.C.

    White House   White Home   Congress

Bingo

1. Make your bingo card.
Your teacher reads a word or phrase. Choose any square and write the word or phrase inside that square. Write one word or phrase in each square. Don't fill in the squares in order.

2. Check your spelling.
The teacher writes the words on the board. Find the correct spelling of each word and check your card. Correct any mistakes.

3. Play bingo.
The teacher reads a clue. Find the square containing the word or phrase that has the same meaning as the teacher's clue. Cover the square with a marker. When you have three covered squares in a row, you have BINGO!

Get It Together

There is a word missing in each sentence below. Choose the correct word from the word list.
Print that word in the boxes of the puzzle.

legislative Court vice
eagle stars stripes
White House senator
president red executive
judge

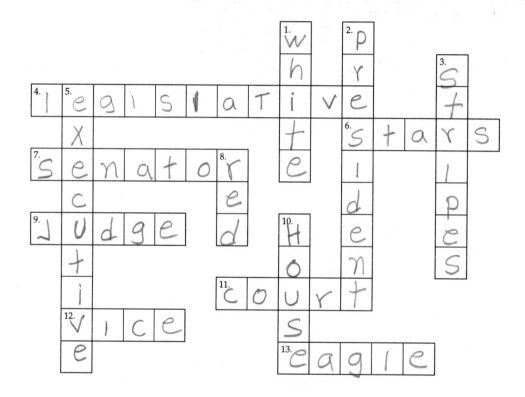

Across

4. The _____ branch makes the laws.

6. There are 50 _____ on the flag.

7. A _____ works in the Senate.

9. A _____ works in the Supreme Court.

11. The Supreme _____ is in the judicial branch.

12. The _____ -president helps the president.

13. The _____ is a national emblem.

Down

1. The president lives in the __Red__ House.

2. The first _____ was George Washington.

3. There are 13 _____ on the flag.

5. The president is in the _____ branch.

8. The flag colors are _____, white, and blue.

10. The president lives in the White _____ .

Unit
5

SHOPPING FOR FOOD

Picture It

The following pictures show people and things that will be discussed in this unit. Refer to these pictures when doing exercises throughout the unit.

1._____ 2._____ 3._____

1._____ 3._____ 5._____

2._____ 4._____

1._____

2._____

_____

3._____

4._____

5._____

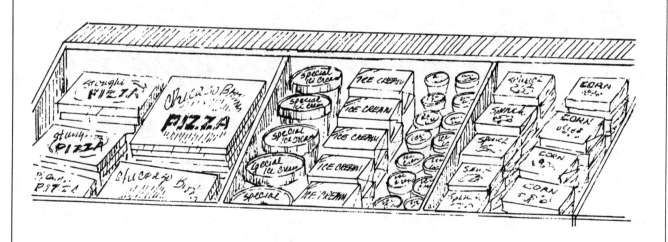

6._____

7._____

8._____

9._____

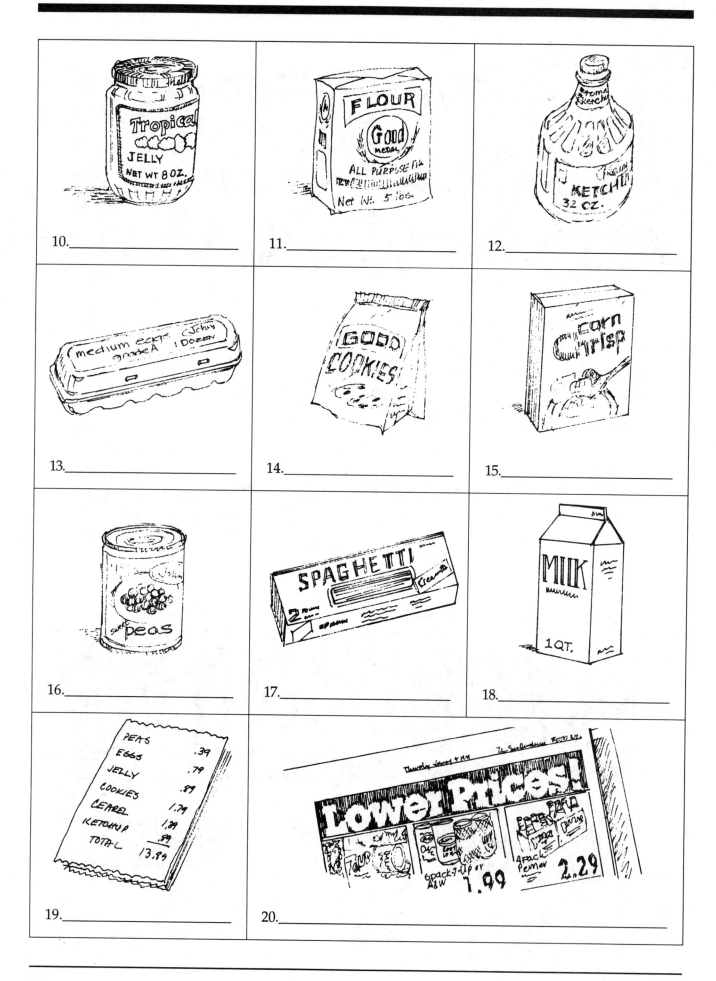

10._____

11._____

12._____

13._____

14._____

15._____

16._____

17._____

18._____

19._____

20._____

Give It a Try

Follow the teacher's instructions to practice the phrases below.

1. Is <u>cereal</u> on sale today? Yes, it's 10% off.

    rice
    flour

2. Where is the <u>canned fruit</u>? It's on aisle 3.

        spaghetti
        soup
        hot sauce

3. I have to return this <u>milk</u>. It's spoiled.

          cheese
          butter
          fish

4. The <u>cashier</u> works until <u>7:00</u> tonight. How late <u>do you</u> work?

    manager   7:30   does Rosa
    clerk   10:00   does Patrick

5. The <u>tomatoes</u> are in the <u>produce section</u>.

    napkins   paper products section
    chicken   meat section
    donuts   bakery

6. Where is the <u>produce section</u>?

        paper products section
        meat section
        bakery

7. I'm going to the <u>beverage</u> section. I need <u>a soda</u>.

        dairy   milk
        frozen food   ice cream
        meat   hamburger

8. I bought a <u>box</u> of <u>peas</u>.

      can   corn
      bottle   ketchup
      jar   jelly

Attention, Please!

Listen to the teacher's cue. Then, circle the correct response.

1. eggs   flour   soup

2. bread   coffee   cereal

3. eggs   crackers   milk

4. spaghetti   oranges   apples

5. potato chips   soup   bread

6. apples   orange juice   jelly

7. milk   orange juice   hamburger

8. orange juice   coffee   bread

9. cottage cheese eggs   butter

10. carrots   milk   cereal

11. napkins   oil   bread

12. butter   ketchup   flour

Tell Me About It (Part A)

Study the picture. Then, ask your partner the questions below. Using your partner's answers, write the name and price of each underlined item in the correct place on the picture.

Where's the <u>flour</u>?   How much is the <u>flour</u>?
Where's the <u>oatmeal</u>?   How much is the <u>oatmeal</u>?
Where's the <u>rice</u>?   How much is the <u>rice</u>?
Where's the <u>coffee</u>?   How much is the <u>coffee</u>?
Where's the <u>cereal</u>?   How much is the <u>cereal</u>?
What's on sale today?

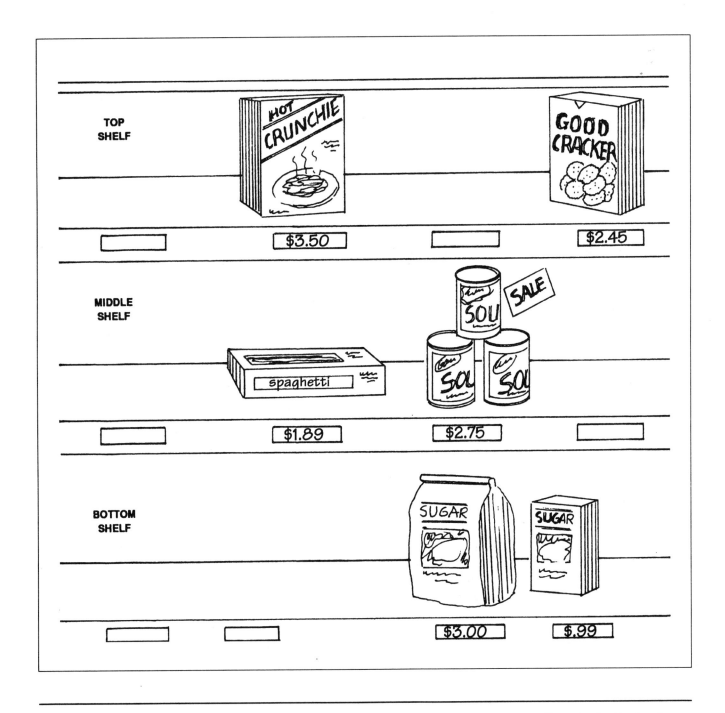

Tell Me About It (Part B)

Study the picture. Then, ask your partner the questions below. Using your partner's answers, write the name and price of each underlined item in the correct place on the picture.

Where's the <u>soup</u>?

Where's the <u>spaghetti</u>?

Where's the <u>sugar</u>?

Where's the <u>hot cereal</u>?

Where are the <u>crackers</u>?

What's on sale today?

How much is the <u>soup</u>?

How much is the <u>spaghetti</u>?

How much is the <u>sugar</u>?

How much is the <u>hot cereal</u>?

How much are the <u>crackers</u>?

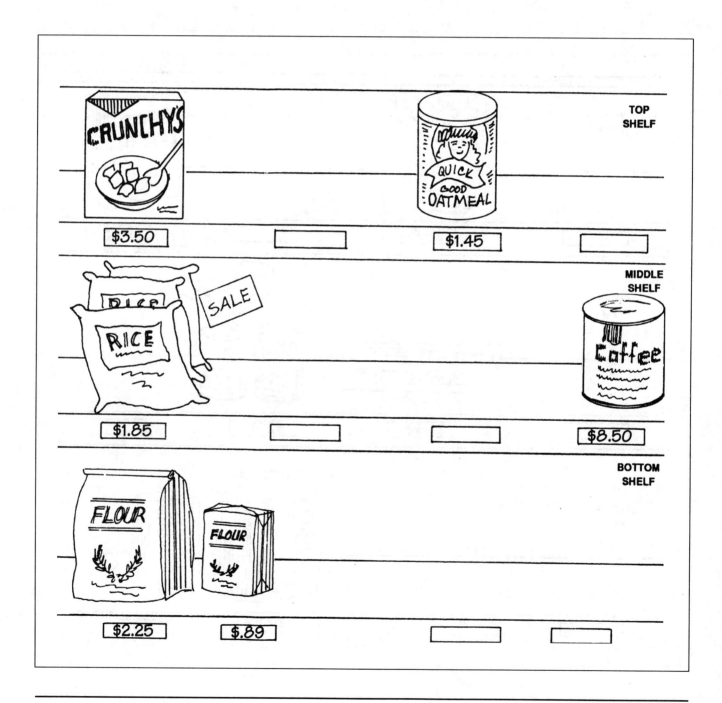

Guess Who, Where, or What

Read each word or phrase in the list below. Ask a classmate if the word or phrase describes a person, place, or thing. Write the words in the correct category.

cashier   manager   produce

milk   deli   bakery

eggs   flour   rice

meats   frozen foods   sugar

canned foods   paper products   napkins

bagger   butcher   dairy

oranges   butter

People Who Work in the Supermarket	Sections of the Supermarket	Things to Buy at the Supermarket

Two Against One

Circle the word that doesn't belong to the set. Explain your choice.

1. oranges   apples   chicken

2. turkey   soup   hamburger

3. milk   carrots   butter

4. milk   bread   rolls

5. lb.   oz.   quart

6. bottle   carton   apples

7. cashier   express lane   check-out stand

8. dairy   lettuce   bakery

9. coffee   potatoes   tea

10. lettuce   celery   rice

11. shopping cart   bag   sack

12. napkins   can of peas   paper products

Inside Story

Read the story below. Choose words or phrases from the list that have the same meanings as the words or phrases under the lines. Write the correct words on the blanks. Read the story again using the words written on the blanks.

cashier	bags	sale
dairy	shopping	hungry
pounds	bakery	supermarket
40	produce	check-out lane
groceries	list	shopping cart

Shopping with Kien

Kien needed _____ , so he went _____
(food)   (to buy food)

after work. When Kien went inside the _____ he noticed that he forgot his
(food store)

_____ . He thought he could remember what he needed.
(notes)

Kien walked to the _____ section and put apples, oranges, and carrots
(fruit and vegetable)

in his _____ . Then he went to the _____ for
(basket)   (bread section)

bread, the _____ section for cheese and to the meat section for two
(milk products)

_____ of hamburger.
(lbs.)

There was a _____ on ice cream and on pizza. Kien didn't need ice
(bargain)

cream or pizza, but he was _____ . After _____
(starving)   (forty)

minutes, Kien was tired. He went to the _____ with a full cart.
(cashier's lane)

The _____ worked fast. Kien's bill was $43.16. Four
(clerk)

_____ of groceries! Kien decided not to forget his list next time!
(bags)

Take Your Pick

There is a missing word or phrase in each sentence below. Read each sentence. Then, look at the three choices under the sentence. Choose the correct word or phrase and write it on the blank.

1. Angela _____ at Star Market once a week.

   shops   shopping   buys

2. The cereal is _____ the top shelf.

   in   on   over

3. Mark needs two _____ of milk.

   quarters   quarts   quart

4. They had a _____ at Michael's Grocery Store.

   sale   sell   sail

5. Tomas, what will you _____ at the sale?

   buy   by   bye

6. Do you have a _____ ?

   buy   shopping   receipt

7. Cathy bought two _____ of hamburger.

   boxes   pounds   cartons

8. The _____ foods are on aisle #3.

   shopping   canned   quart

9. Kim went _____ after work.

   shop   shopping   shopped

10. The express lane _____ fast.

   is   are   were

Bingo

1. Make your bingo card.
Your teacher reads a word or phrase. Choose any square and write the word or phrase inside that square. Write one word or phrase in each square. Don't fill in the squares in order.

2. Check your spelling.
The teacher writes the words on the board. Find the correct spelling of each word and check your card. Correct any mistakes.

3. Play bingo.
The teacher reads a clue. Find the square containing the word or phrase that has the same meaning as the teacher's clue. Cover the square with a marker. When you have three covered squares in a row, you have BINGO!

Get It Together

There is a word missing in each sentence below. Choose the correct word from the word list. Print that word in the boxes of the puzzle.

tomatoes   supermarket   frozen
bakery   list   dairy
lane   deli   sale
out   in   aisle

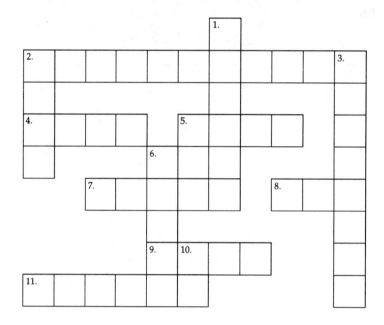

Across

2. Buy food at the _____ .

4. Only seven items at the express _____ .

5. Buy sandwiches at the _____ .

7. Buy milk in the _____ section.

8. The sign on the exit says _____ .

9. Make a shopping _____ .

11. The _____ pizza is cold.

Down

1. Buy bread at the _____ .

2. There's a big _____ today.

3. The _____ are in the produce section.

6. The canned fruit is on _____ 3.

10. The sign on the entrance says _____ .

Unit
6

SHOPPING FOR CLOTHING

Picture It

The following pictures show people and things that will be discussed in this unit. Refer to these pictures when doing exercises throughout the unit.

1._____   4._____   7._____

2._____   5._____

3._____   6._____

1._____

2._____

3._____

4._____

5.

6._____

7._____

8._____

9._____

10._____

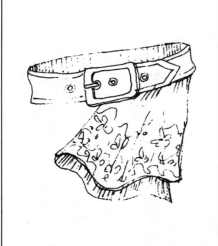

11._____

12._____

13._____

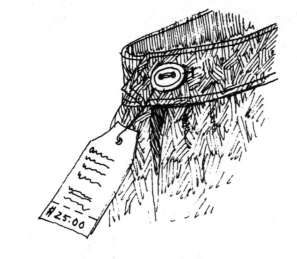

14._____

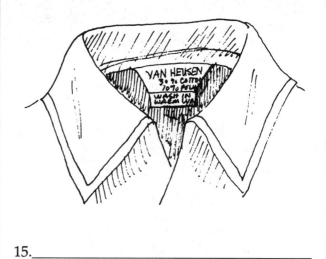

15._____

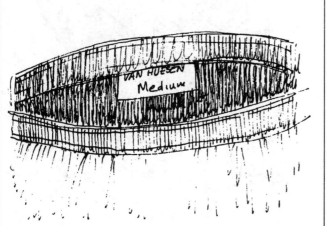

16._____

17._____

18._____

19._____

20._____

21._____

22._____

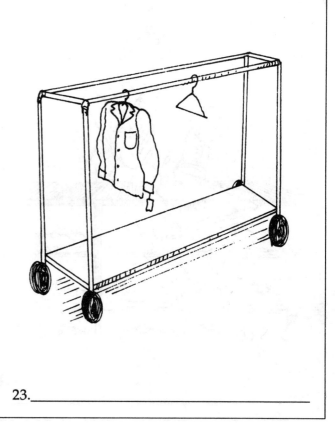

23._____

Give It a Try

Follow the teacher's instructions to practice the phrases below.

1. The _blouse_ is too small. Why don't you _exchange it_?

    skirt   return it
    shirt   take it back
    sweater   give it back

2. I'd like that ___shirt___ in a size _15-1/2 by 34_.

        belt   32
        nightgown   6 or a small
        hat   7-1/4
        dress   12
        jacket   38 regular

3. Where is the _women's clothing_ department? It's _straight ahead_.

      men's clothing   on the third floor
      jewelry   over there
      accessories   in the basement
      children's clothing   upstairs

4. He needs a new pair of _shoes_, but these are too _big_.

        jeans   tight
        pajamas   long
        shorts   small
        socks   large

5. How much is the _robe_? It's ___$17.99___.

      jacket $34.50
      dress $29.95 on sale
      coat $45.00
      belt $16.75 plus tax

6. The ___suits___ are in the ___men's clothing___ section.

    belts   accessories
    necklaces   jewelry
    bibs   children's clothing
    blouses   women's clothing

Attention, Please!

Listen to the teacher's cue. Then, circle the correct response.

1. aisle #2   fitting room   jewelry department

2. jewelry   coats   scarf

3. small   medium   large

4. accessories   jewelry   men's clothing

5. men's clothing   women's clothing   shoe department

6. sell   exchange   receipt

7. department   cashier   discount

8. small   medium   large

9. bag of shirts   price of shirts   rack of shirts

10. sell   give   return

11. care label   price tag   size

12. shoes   sizes   department

Tell Me About It (Part A)

Study the picture. Then, ask your partner the questions below. Using your partner's answers, write the name, price, and/or size of each underlined item in the correct place on the picture.

How much are the <u>hats</u>?

How much are the <u>sweaters</u>?

How much are the <u>shorts</u>?

How much are the <u>belts</u>?

What's the <u>"summer special"</u>?

Tell Me About It (Part B)

Study the picture. Then, ask your partner the questions below. Using your partner's answers, write the name, price, and/or size of each underlined item in the correct place on the picture.

How much are the <u>skirts</u>?

How much are the <u>socks</u>?

What sizes are the <u>jackets</u>?

What's the <u>special</u>?

Is the <u>jewelry</u> on sale?

Guess Who, Where, or What

Read each word or phrase in the list below. Ask a classmate if the word or phrase describes a person, place, or thing. Write the words in the correct category.

manager
children's clothing
tie
dress
pants
shoe department
fitting room
blouse

hat
jewelry department
bracelet
men's clothing department
customer
cashier
socks

coat
clerk
scarf
accessories department
assistant manager
sweater
women's clothing department

People Seen at a Department Store	Places in a Department Store	Things to Buy in a Department Store

Two Against One

Circle the word that doesn't belong to the set. Explain your choice.

1. women's clothing   men's clothing   hat

2. gloves   hat   pajamas

3. socks   dress   stockings

4. dress   underwear   slip

5. belt   shoes   socks

6. dress   skirt   tie

7. jacket   robe   coat

8. skirt   watch   pants

9. nightgown   bracelet   necklace

10. coat   sweater   shorts

11. jewelry   belt   bracelet

12. accessories   gloves   suits

Inside Story

Read the story below. Choose words or phrases from the list that have the same meanings as the words or phrases under the lines. Write the correct words on the blanks. Read the story again using the words written on the blanks.

little	jeans	eight
big	discount	start
$12.00	right	fast
department	sales	ad
children's	racks	

Rena's Shopping Trip

Rena's daughter, Joanna, is _____ years old. She is growing
(8)

_____ . Joanna is going back to school in September, and she needs some
(quickly)

new clothes.

Rena decided to go to Brown's _____ store for the back-to-school
(low cost)

_____ . She saw an _____ in the weekend
(bargains)   (advertisement)

paper. Everything was on sale!

The _____ clothing _____ was crowded.
(young people's)   (section)

The _____ were only $9.50. The sweaters were
(denim pants)

_____ . There were two _____ of skirts on sale.
(twelve dollars)   (bars)

Rena didn't know where to _____ .
(begin)

Rena held up a sweater. Is this too _____ ? Rena held up a skirt. Is
(large)

this too _____ ? It was hard to guess the _____ size.
(small)   (correct)

Rena had to bring Joanna back to the store to try on the clothes.

Take Your Pick

There is a missing word or phrase in each sentence below. Read each sentence. Then, look at the three choices under the sentence. Choose the correct word or phrase and write it on the blank.

1. The shirts _____ on sale yesterday.

   was   is   were

2. The blouses are _____ sale today.

   in   on   under

3. John is looking for the men's _____ .

   cloth department   clothings department   clothing department

4. He wore his new _____ last night.

   pajamas   pajama   pajama's

5. Carlos needed to _____ the suit.

   try in   try out   try on

6. Where is the_____ department?

   jewels   jewelry   jewelries

7. Karim is in the _____ room.

   fitting   fit   fitted

8. Molly wants to _____ the sweater. It's too big.

   change   exchange   fitting

9. The blouse is _____ big.

   to   too   two

10. Sein needs a sweater to _____ the pants.

    match   matches   matching

Bingo

1. Make your bingo card.
Your teacher reads a word or phrase. Choose any square and write the word or phrase inside that square. Write one word or phrase in each square. Don't fill in the squares in order.

2. Check your spelling.
The teacher writes the words on the board. Find the correct spelling of each word and check your card. Correct any mistakes.

3. Play bingo.
The teacher reads a clue. Find the square containing the word or phrase that has the same meaning as the teacher's clue. Cover the square with a marker. When you have three covered squares in a row, you have BINGO!

Get It Together

There is a word missing in each sentence below. Choose the correct word from the word list. Print that word in the boxes of the puzzle.

ad
suit
medium
shopping
small

large
tie
sales
department
need

pants
aisles
shirt
men

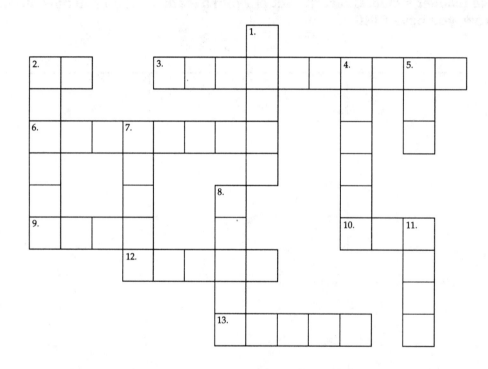

Across

2. The _____ is in the newspaper.

3. Buy clothes at a _____ store.

6. Take a _____ list to the store.

9. He wore a _____ and tie.

10. The shirts on aisle 2 are for _____ , not

    women.

12. The dress is tight. It's too _____ .

13. The _____ is size 12.

Down

1. The hat is very big. It's size _____ .

2. The children's clothing section is on

    _____ 3 and 4.

4. The shirt is not large or small. It's _____ .

5. He wore a coat and _____ .

7. He wore a pair of _____ .

8. The store has many _____ today.

11. You _____ some new clothes.

Unit
7

TRANSPORTATION

Picture It

The following pictures show people and things that will be discussed in this unit. Refer to these pictures when doing exercises throughout the unit.

1._____   3._____   5._____

2._____   4._____   6._____

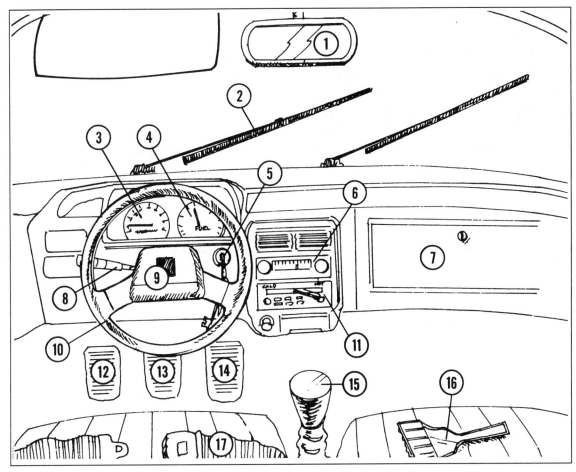

1._____ 7._____ 13._____

2._____ 8._____ 14._____

3._____ 9._____ 15._____

4._____ 10._____ 16._____

5._____ 11._____ 17._____

6._____ 12._____

1._____

2._____

3._____

4._____

5._____

1._____

2._____

3._____

4._____

5._____

6._____

7._____

8._____

9._____

10._____

11._____

12._____

Give It a Try

Follow the teacher's instructions to practice the phrases below.

1. Would you check the __oil__ , please? _____Certainly_____.

                      tires   Of course.
                      battery   I'd be glad to.
                      brakes   What's the problem?
                      clutch   I'm sorry, I can't right now.

2. Did the mechanic fix the _speedometer_ ? _Yes, she did_ .

                        brakes
                        ignition
                        gear shift   No, she didn't.

3. The _gas gauge_ isn't working. The _____brakes_____ aren't working.

     turn signal   lights
     radio   windshield wipers

4. There's a _mechanic_ on duty, isn't there? Yes, there is.

                bus driver
                taxi driver

5. I need a gas station with a _self service pump_ .

                        carwash
                        garage
                        restroom

6. Is the _taxi_ late? _Yes, it's 30 minutes late_ .

     bus
     plane
     train   No, it's early.

7. Where's the _garage_ ? In the _____main square_____.

              map   glove compartment
              jack   trunk
               car   garage

8. He uses _____regular gas_____ in the _truck_ .

          unleaded gas   taxi
          diesel fuel   bus

Attention, Please!

Listen to the teacher's cue. Then, circle the correct response.

1. steering wheel   brake   gas pedal

2. tires   trunk   key

3. glove compartment   radio   ignition

4. radio   glove compartment   clutch

5. brakes   key   gear shift

6. speedometer   key   gas gauge

7. ignition   radio   gear shift

8. gas gauge   trunk   window

9. battery   radio   lights

10. gas tank   speedometer   seatbelt

11. brakes   seatbelt   trunk

12. horn   tires   key

Tell Me About It (Part A)

Study the picture. Then, ask your partner the questions below. Using your partner's answers, write the name of each underlined item in the correct place on the picture.

Where's the <u>speedometer</u>?

Where's the <u>clutch</u>?

Where's the <u>glove box</u>?

Where's the <u>visor</u>?

Where's the <u>gas pedal</u>?

Where's the <u>heater</u>?

Where are the <u>windshield wipers</u>?

Where's the <u>seatbelt</u>?

Tell Me About It (Part B)

Study the picture. Then, ask your partner the questions below. Using your partner's answers, write the name of each underlined item in the correct place on the picture.

Where's the <u>radio</u>?

Where's the <u>rear view mirror</u>?

Where are the <u>lights</u>?

Where's the <u>brake</u>?

Where's the <u>turn signal</u>?

Where's the <u>gas gauge</u>?

Where's the <u>ignition</u>?

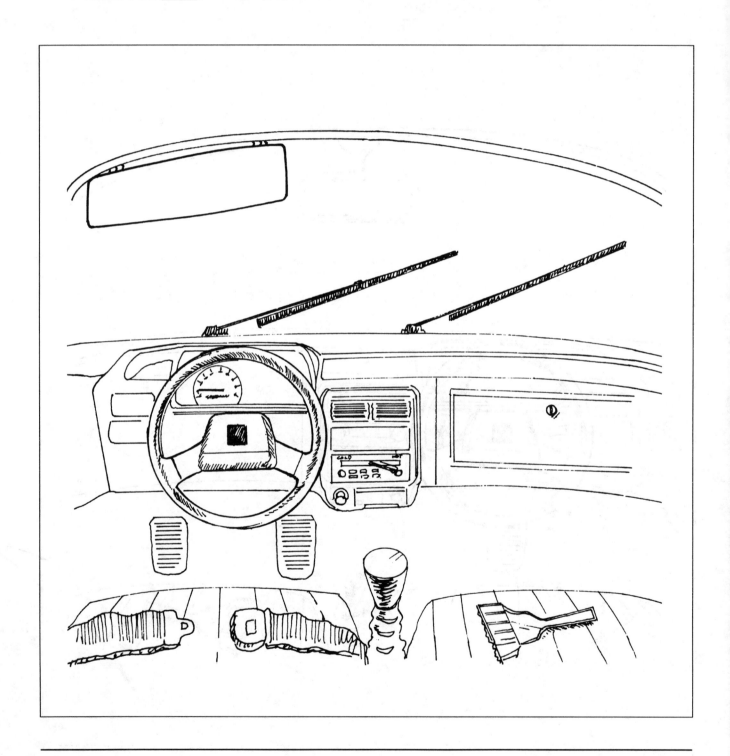

Guess Who, Where, or What

Read each word or phrase in the list below. Ask a classmate if the word or phrase describes a person, place, or thing. Write the words in the correct category.

bus driver   bus station   steering wheel
airport   gear shift   pilot
cab driver   train station   glove box
mechanic   garage   speedometer
gas gauge   station attendant   carwash
visor   truck driver   seatbelt
flight attendant   bus stop   ignition
police officer   gas pedal   turn signal

People Who Work in Transportation	Transportation Places	Things Inside a Car

Two Against One

Circle the word that doesn't belong to the set. Explain your choice.

1. car   bus   plane

2. bus station   bicycle   airport

3. truck   plane   bus

4. pilot   plane   car

5. gear shift   speedometer   driver

6. lights   battery   radio

7. scraper   brakes   clutch

8. tire   horn   turn signal

9. seatbelt   bus   train

10. gasoline   oil   car

11. ignition   tires   turn signal

12. airport   bus driver   taxi driver

Inside Story

Read the story below. Choose words or phrases from the list that have the same meanings as the words or phrases under the lines. Write the correct words on the blanks. Read the story again using the words written on the blanks.

- battery
- horn
- gas pedal
- dashboard
- windshield
- morning

- service station
- lights
- ignition
- radio
- seatbelt

- driver's seat
- got out of
- clutch
- start
- scraper

A Cold Morning for Juan

It was a very cold December _____ . Juan used his

(A.M.)

_____ to clean the ice from his _____ . He got

(cleaner)   (front car window)

into the _____ , fastened the _____ , and put

(seat behind the wheel)   (belt)

the key into the _____ .

(starter)

The lights on the _____ were red, but the car didn't

(panel)

_____ . Juan put in the _____ and stepped on

(turn on)   (pedal on the left)

the _____ . He turned the key again. Nothing. Only a rumble.

(pedal on the right)

Now what? Juan tried the _____ . They didn't work. Juan tried the

(lamps)

_____ . It didn't work. Juan tried the _____ .

(honker)   (music player)

It didn't work.

"The _____ ! It's too old. It's too cold," he exclaimed. Juan

(electric current box)

_____ the car and called a _____ .

(exited)   (gas station)

Take Your Pick

There is a missing word or phrase in each sentence below. Read each sentence. Then, look at the three choices under the sentence. Choose the correct word or phrase and write it on the blank.

1. Juan missed the bus, so he took a _____ to work.

   taxi   ticket   pilot

2. The flight was _____ , so Margarita couldn't go at all.

   late   early   cancelled

3. The _____ was so crowded, Maria missed her flight.

   airport   bus station   train station

4. The _____ missed the turn on 5th Street.

   pilot   attendant   bus driver

5. She got a ticket because she was _____ without a license.

   flying   driving   drive

6. Margo took her car to the _____ to be fixed.

   garage   carwash   airport

7. When Juanita passed the test, she got her _____ .

   driver's license   traffic license   mother's license

8. Mario borrowed Juan's _____ to move his heavy furniture.

   bicycle   train   truck

9. Step on the _____ !

   speedometer   brakes   ignition

10. Don't forget to fasten your _____ .

    seatbelt   steering wheel   windows

Bingo

1. Make your bingo card.
Your teacher reads a word or phrase. Choose any square and write the word or phrase inside that square. Write one word or phrase in each square. Don't fill in the squares in order.

2. Check your spelling.
The teacher writes the words on the board. Find the correct spelling of each word and check your card. Correct any mistakes.

3. Play bingo.
The teacher reads a clue. Find the square containing the word or phrase that has the same meaning as the teacher's clue. Cover the square with a marker. When you have three covered squares in a row, you have BINGO!

Get It Together

There is a word missing in each sentence below. Choose the correct word from the word list. Print that word in the boxes of the puzzle.

seatbelt   restroom   speedometer   can
cashier   horn   gas   mechanic
full   wash   license   radio
pedal   key

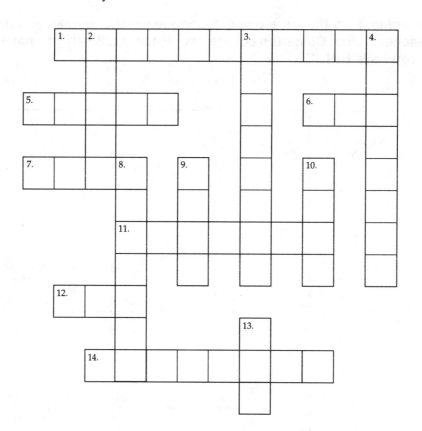

Across

1. The _____ reads 65 mph.

5. The _____ plays music.

6. The gauge says "E." I need _____ .

7. The gauge says "F." It means _____ .

11. Pay the _____ .

12. Put the paper in the trash _____ .

14. Fasten your _____ .

Down

2. Step on the gas _____ .

3. The _____ fixes cars.

4. He's in the men's _____ .

8. I need to see your registration and your

    driver's _____ .

9. The car is dirty. Go to the car _____ .

10. Honk the _____ .

13. Put the _____ in the ignition.

Unit 8

COMMUNITY SERVICES

Picture It

The following pictures show people and things that will be discussed in this unit. Refer to these pictures when doing exercises throughout the unit.

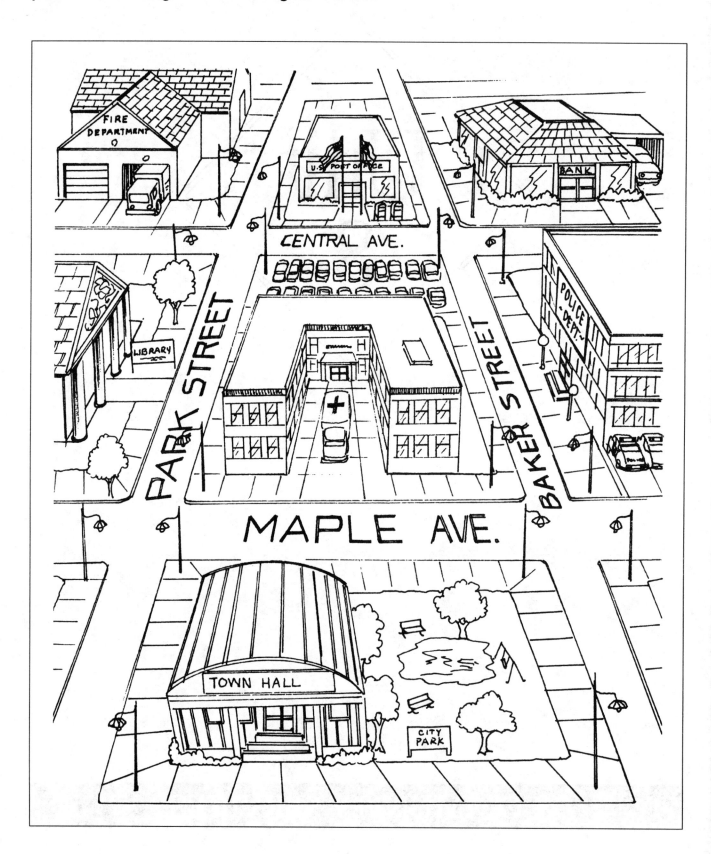

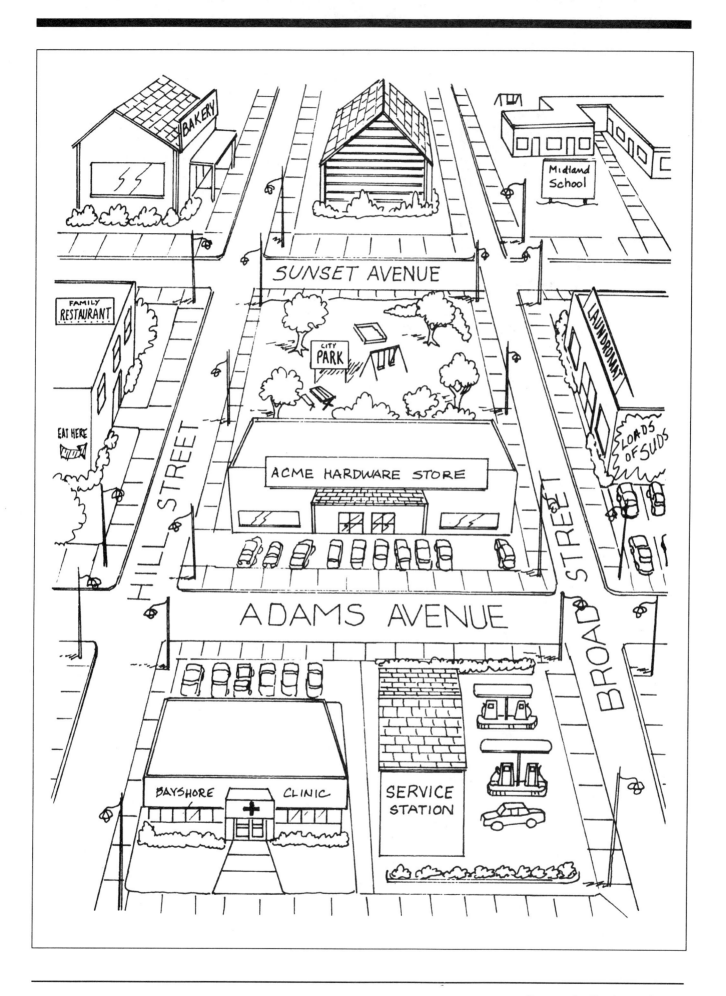

1._____

2._____

3._____

4._____

5._____

6._____

7._____

8._____

9._____

10._____

11._____

12._____

Give It a Try

Follow the teacher's instructions to practice the phrases below.

1. The ___bank___ is closed on Sunday.
   > post office
   > clinic
   > town hall

2. The ___bakery___ is open on Sunday.
   > service station
   > library
   > laundromat
   > hospital

3. Where is the _police department_?
   > fire department
   > service station
   > hardware store

4. The ___school___ is on the corner of 5th Street and Baker Street.
   > laundromat
   > restaurant
   > post office

5. The _librarian_ works at the ___library___ until 4:00 P.M.
   > teller   bank
   > cashier   hardware store
   > doctor   clinic

6. _Police officers_ work on Sunday.
   > Waiters
   > Librarians
   > Fire fighters

7. The _service station attendant_ takes your money.
   > cashier
   > store clerk
   > teller

Attention, Please!

Listen to the teacher's cue. Then, circle the correct response.

1. police officer   librarian   baker

2. mail carrier   teller   fire fighter

3. teacher   sales clerk   service station

4. librarian   teacher   doctor

5. police department   library   school

6. bakery   post office   laundromat

7. laundromat   school   hardware store

8. post office   bank   bakery

9. park   service station   fire department

10. books   stamps   letters

11. books   letters   classes

12. corner   street   clinic

Tell Me About It (Part A)

Study the picture. Then, ask your partner the questions below. Using your partner's answers, write the name of each underlined item in the correct place on the picture.

Where's the <u>hardware store</u>?　　　　Where's the <u>town hall</u>?
Where's the <u>library</u>?　　　　　　　Where's the <u>fire department</u>?
Where's the <u>clinic</u>?　　　　　　　Where's the <u>post office</u>?
Where's the <u>restaurant</u>?　　　　　Where's the <u>bakery</u>?

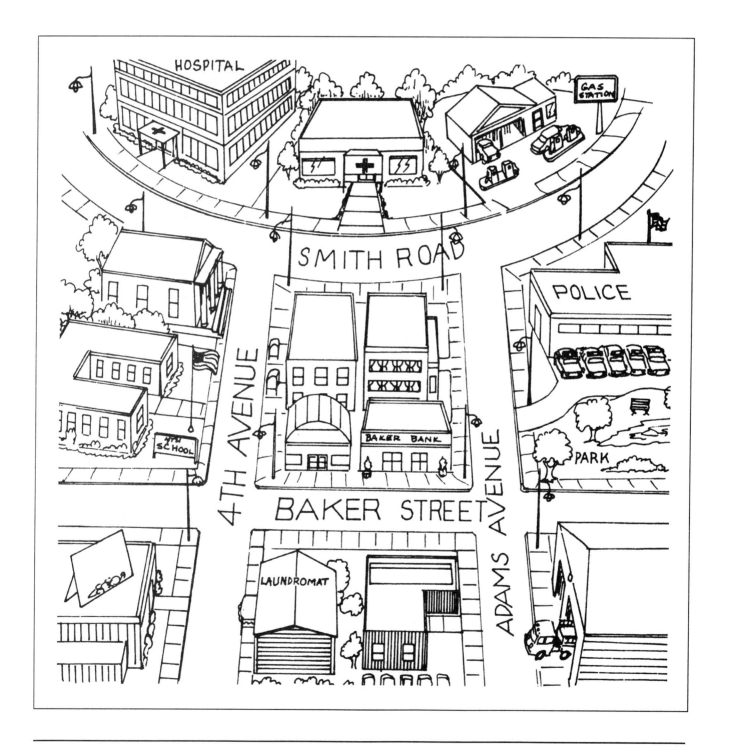

Tell Me About It (Part B)

Study the picture. Then, ask your partner the questions below. Using your partner's answers, write the name of each underlined item in the correct place on the picture.

Where's the <u>school</u>?

Where's the <u>hospital</u>?

Where's the <u>laundromat</u>?

Where's the <u>bank</u>?

Where's the <u>park</u>?

Where's the <u>police department</u>?

Where's the <u>service station</u>?

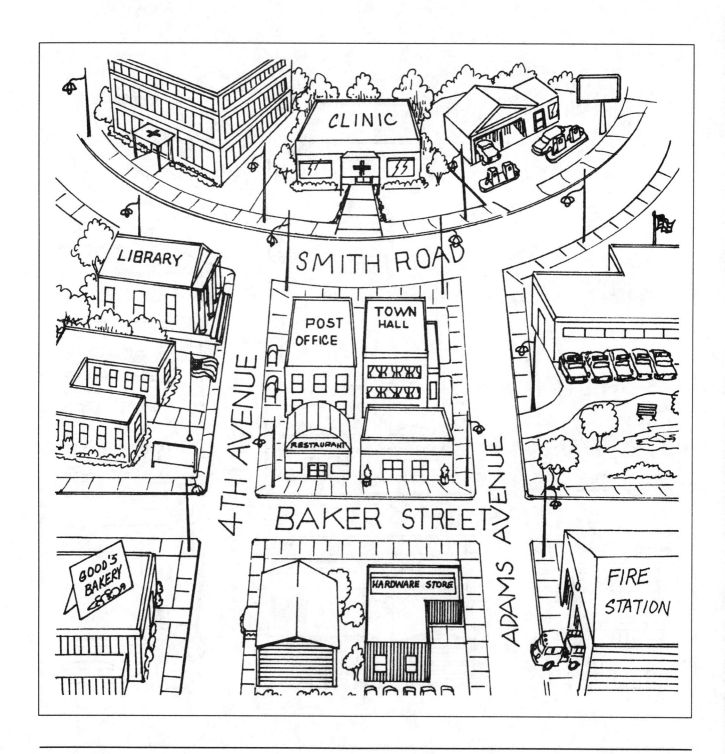

Guess Who, Where, or What

Read each word or phrase in the list below. Ask a classmate if the word or phrase describes a person, place, or thing. Write the words in the correct category.

teller

post office

X-ray

doctor

town hall

books

clinic

nurse

stamps

bank

park

gasoline

hospital

waitress

deposit

accident report

police officer

mail carrier

service station

cashier

library

fire department

physical exam

breakfast

librarian

hammer and nails

People Working in Community Services	Community Services	Services Provided

Two Against One

Circle the word that doesn't belong to the set. Explain your choice.

1. fire fighter   fire department   mail

2. bread   books   baker

3. teller   classes   school

4. library   post office   mail carrier

5. teller   town hall   bank

6. nurse   hospital   clerk

7. avenue   school   street

8. corner   emergency   hospital

9. bank   check   police officer

10. hardware store   park   cashier

11. letters   stamps   post office

12. hammer   laundromat   hardware store

Inside Story

Read the story below. Choose words or phrases from the list that have the same meanings as the words or phrases under the lines. Write the correct words on the blanks. Read the story again using the words written on the blanks.

buy	make a deposit	2:30
clinic	return	service station
police department	tired	Then
errands to run	mail	Tuesday
an appointment	books	clothes

Kim's Errands

Kim had many _____ on _____ . She had
　　　　　　　　　　(places to go)　　　　　　　　　　　(Tues.)

to go to the post office to _____ stamps and
　　　　　　　　　　　　　　　　　(purchase)

_____ a package. _____ , she had to go to the
　　　　(send)　　　　　　　　　　　　　　　　(After that)

bank to _____ . Then, to the library to _____
　　　(put money into her account)　　　　　　　　　　　　　　　(take back)

some _____ . Then, to the _____ . Her son,
　　　(reading material)　　　　　　　　　　　(health-care facility)

Kien, had _____ at _____ .
　　　　　(a visit time)　　　　　　　　(two-thirty)

She also had to fill her car at the _____ , wash a load of
　　　　　　　　　　　　　　　　　　(gas station)

_____ at the laundromat, and buy a bike license at the
　　(laundry)

_____ .
　　(police station)

What a busy day! She was _____ just thinking about it!
　　　　　　　　　　　　　　　(exhausted)

Take Your Pick

There is a missing word or phrase in each sentence below. Read each sentence. Then, look at the three choices under the sentence. Choose the correct word or phrase and write it on the blank.

1. The _____ works at the bakery.

   baker   bake   bread

2. A mail carrier _____ mail to your house.

   delivery   delivers   deliver

3. The _____ cashes checks at the bank.

   teller   tell   told

4. Jose went to the _____ for an accident report.

   department police   police   police department

5. I want to _____ this book.

   check out   check around   check over

6. Where _____ the laundromat?

   are   were   is

7. What time does the library _____ ?

   close   closed   closing

8. The police _____ stopped the car.

   office   department   officer

9. The park is _____ the corner of 5th Street and James Avenue.

   in   over   on

10. Farid went to the service station to _____ his car with gas.

    fill   full   filled

Bingo

1. Make your bingo card.
Your teacher reads a word or phrase. Choose any square and write the word or phrase inside that square. Write one word or phrase in each square. Don't fill in the squares in order.

2. Check your spelling.
The teacher writes the words on the board. Find the correct spelling of each word and check your card. Correct any mistakes.

3. Play bingo.
The teacher reads a clue. Find the square containing the word or phrase that has the same meaning as the teacher's clue. Cover the square with a marker. When you have three covered squares in a row, you have BINGO!

Get It Together

There is a word missing in each sentence below. Choose the correct word from the word list. Print that word in the boxes of the puzzle.

restaurant   park   library   laundromat
clinic   avenue   corner   fire
school   bank   service   out
bakery

Across

1. He takes English classes at _____ .

4. Eat lunch at the _____ .

5. Call the _____ department for emergencies.

7. The bank is on the _____ of 5th and Hill St.

9. The abbreviation for _____ is ave.

10. They had a picnic in the _____ .

11. Return the books to the _____ .

Down

1. Buy gasoline at the _____ station.

2. They're going _____ for lunch.

3. Wash clothes at the _____ .

6. He made a deposit at the _____ .

7. He has an appointment at the _____ .

8. Buy bread at the _____ .

Unit 9

MONEY AND BANKING

Picture It

The following pictures show people and things that will be discussed in this unit. Refer to these pictures when doing exercises throughout the unit.

1._____   3._____

2._____   4._____

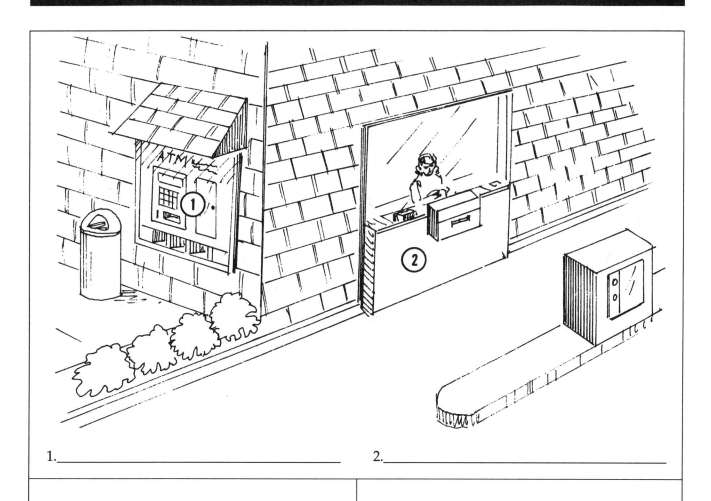

1._____

2._____

3._____

4._____

5._____

6._____

7._____

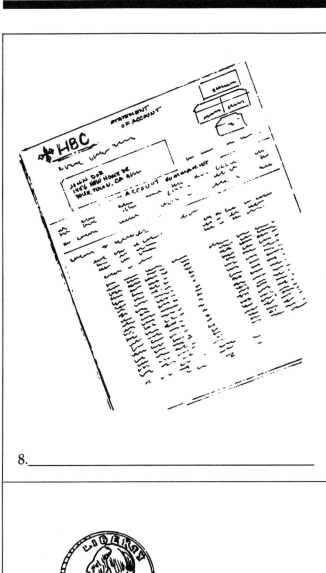

8._____

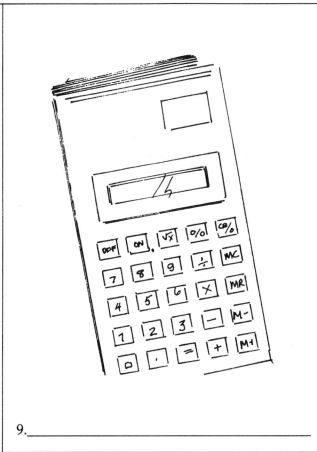

9._____

10._____

11._____

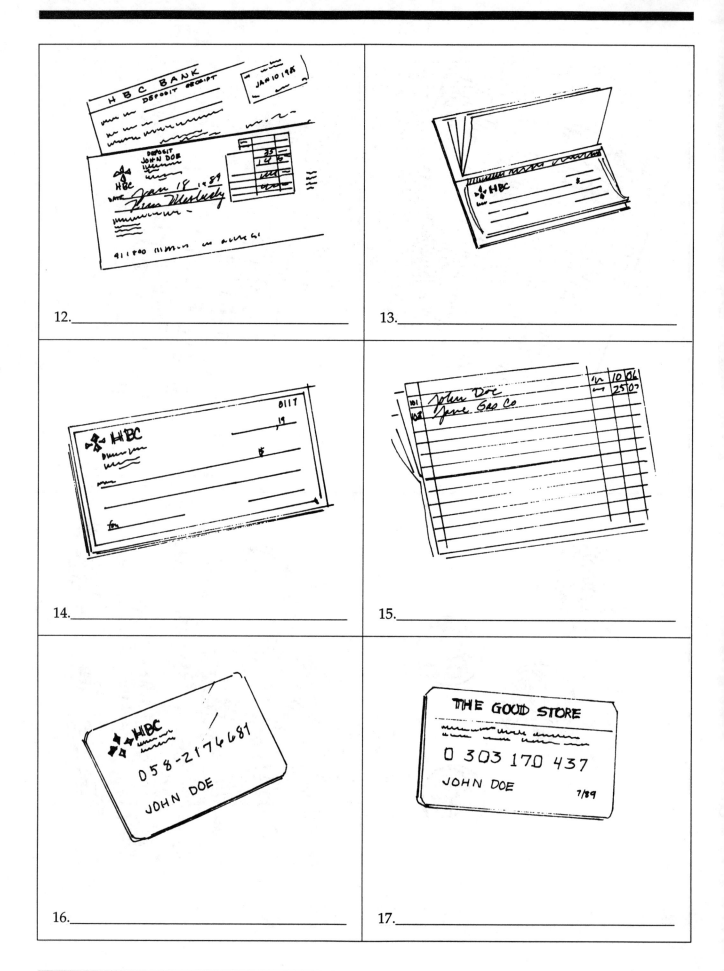

12. _____

13. _____

14. _____

15. _____

16. _____

17. _____

18._____

19._____

20._____

21._____

22._____

23._____

24._____

25._____

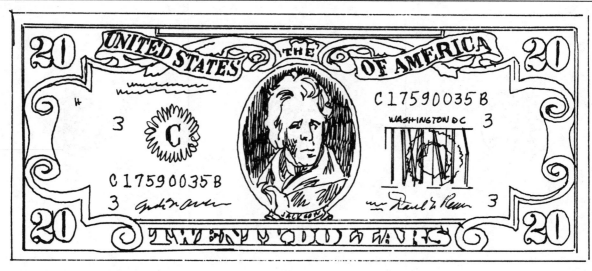

26._____

Give It a Try

Follow the teacher's instructions to practice the phrases below.

1. He wrote a check for $50.00 .

>$25.00
>$42.00
>$12.00
>$15.00

2. She filled out the ___deposit slip___.

>check register
>bank statement
>receipt

3. Add the amounts on the ___calculator___.

>deposit slip
>check register
>bank statement
>receipt

4. Do you have change for ___$1.00___?

>$5.00
>$10.00
>a quarter
>$20.00

5. Pay the bill with ___a check___.

>a credit card
>cash
>bills

6. Don't go inside. Use the ___drive-up window___.

>automatic-teller machine
>night deposit box

7. I lost my _checkbook_.

>ATM card
>credit card
>change

Attention, Please!

Listen to the teacher's cue. Then, circle the correct response.

1. penny   nickel   dime

2. quarter   half dollar   penny

3. $5.75 $5.57 $5.65

4. $15.15 $50.15 $15.50

5. coins   bills   checks

6. check register   withdrawal   deposit

7. bank statement   bank teller   bank account

8. coins   bills   tellers

9. credit card   bank card   note card

10. charge   check   cash

11. 25¢ $1.00   10¢

12. drive-up window   teller   checkbook

Tell Me About It (Part A)

Study the check. Then, ask your partner the questions below. Fill in the check using your partner's answers.

What's the check number?

What's the Matas' address?

Who is the check to?

What's the account number?

Jose or Maria Mata	1809

Date ___March 1___ 19 99

Pay to the order of _____

		350.00

Three Hundred Fifty XX ‖‖‖‖ _____ Dollars

South Bank of San Diego

For ___rent___   Signature *Maria Mata*

Study the deposit slip. Then, ask your partner the questions below. Fill in the deposit slip using your partner's answers.

What's the date?

How many checks are deposited?

What's the name of the bank?

How much is each check for?

For Deposit to the Account of

Jose or Maria Mata
621 Smith Street
San Diego, CA 92128

Date _____ 19 ____

Signature *José Mata*

78/89765-001

CASH	CURRENCY		
	COIN		
CHECKS	1		
	2		
	3		
	4		
TOTAL		490	50
LESS CASH RECEIVED		90	50
NET DEPOSIT		400	00

Tell Me About It (Part B)

Study the check. Then, ask your partner the questions below. Fill in the check using your partner's answers.

What's the date?   How much is the check for?

What's the money for?   Who is writing the check?

Jose or Maria Mata
621 Smith Street
San Diego, CA 92128

1809

Date _____ 19 ____

Pay to the order of *Mr. Carlos Garcia* _____ $ [   ]

_____ Dollars

✸ **South Bank**
of San Diego

For _____   Signature _____

78/89765-001

Study the deposit slip. Then, ask your partner the questions below. Fill in the deposit slip using your partner's answers.

Who is making the deposit?   What's the account number?

What's the total of checks deposited?   How much cash is received?

What's the total deposit?

For Deposit to the Account of

Jose or Maria Mata
621 Smith Street
San Diego, CA 92128

Date *April 30* _____ 19 *99*

Signature _____

✸ **South Bank**
of San Diego

CASH	CURRENCY			
	COIN			
CHECKS	1		420	50
	2		70	00
	3			
	4			
TOTAL				
LESS CASH RECEIVED				
NET DEPOSIT				

Guess Who, Where, or What

Read each word or phrase in the list below. Ask a classmate if the word or phrase describes a person, place, or thing. Write the words in the correct category.

teller
coins
checkbook
office
customer
automatic-teller machine
check

bank manager
drive-up window
receptionist
bank
check register
information desk
deposit slip

safe
security guard
banker
deposit
bills
bank statement
calculator

People in the Bank	Places for Banking	Things in Banking

Two Against One

Circle the word that doesn't belong to the set. Explain your choice.

1. teller   receptionist   safe

2. $5.00 $20.00   49¢

3. deposit slip   bank statement   check register

4. quarter   dime   10¢

5. manager   calculator   security guard

6. drive-up window   automatic-teller machine   deposit

7. check   change   coins

8. credit   deposit   ATM

9. $150.55 $164.20 $137.00

10. Wait Here   cash   Information

11. dollar $1.50 $1.00

12. $ ¢   money

Inside Story

Read the story below. Choose words or phrases from the list that have the same meanings as the words or phrases under the lines. Write the correct words on the blanks. Read the story again using the words written on the blanks.

credit card	$29.00	total
cash	charge	write
checkbook	$15.00	Friday
purse	store	prices
$20.50		

Campan's Shopping Trip

Campan went shopping for some new clothes on _____ . She picked
(Fri.)

out a new dress for _____ , a pair of pants for
(twenty-nine dollars)

_____ , and a pair of shoes for _____ .
(fifteen dollars)   (twenty dollars and fifty cents)

The clerk added the _____ and said, "That
(costs)

_____ is $68.50 with tax. Cash or _____ ?"
(final amount)   (put on account)

Campan said she wanted to _____ a check. She took her
(make out)

_____ out of her _____ . "Oh, no!" she said, "I
(book of checks)   (bag)

used my last check at the other _____ ."
(shop)

The clerk said Campan could use a _____ . Campan didn't have a
(charge card)

credit card, so she had to pay with _____ . She decided it was time to go
(bills and coins)

home.

Take Your Pick

There is a missing word or phrase in each sentence below. Read each sentence. Then, look at the three choices under the sentence. Choose the correct word or phrase and write it on the blank.

1. Waldek wrote a _____ to pay the telephone bill.

   checking   check   checks

2. Do you have _____ for $20.00?

   change   changing   changes

3. Saul filled out the deposit _____ .

   sleep   ship   slip

4. Wait _____ , please.

   here   hear   where

5. Raul used his _____ to total the bill.

   calculation   calculating   calculator

6. They keep money in a _____ .

   save   savings   safe

7. Where is the _____ ?

   security guard   guard security   secure guard

8. Kim used her _____ for I.D.

   ATM check   ATM card   credit card

9. If you don't have much time, go to the _____ .

   drive-up window   drive-in window   drive-around window

10. I have to _____ .

    change a check   check a cash   cash a check

Bingo

1. Make your bingo card.
Your teacher reads a word or phrase. Choose any square and write the word or phrase inside that square. Write one word or phrase in each square. Don't fill in the squares in order.

2. Check your spelling.
The teacher writes the words on the board. Find the correct spelling of each word and check your card. Correct any mistakes.

3. Play bingo.
The teacher reads a clue. Find the square containing the word or phrase that has the same meaning as the teacher's clue. Cover the square with a marker. When you have three covered squares in a row, you have BINGO!

Get It Together

There is a word missing in each sentence below. Choose the correct word from the word list.
Print that word in the boxes of the puzzle.

account	dime	bank	dollar
check	calculator	coin	penny
wait	up	register	three
two	nickels		

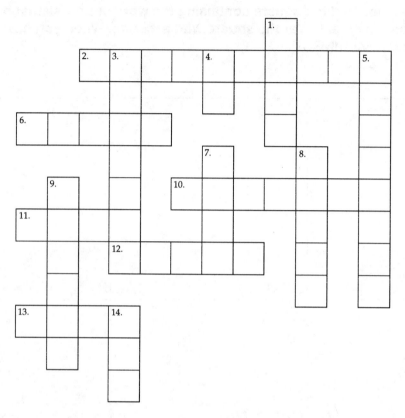

Across

2. Add the amounts on your pocket _____ .

6. I have to write a _____ .

10. One dime is two _____ .

11. A nickel is a _____ .

12. The word for 3 is _____ .

13. _____ here, please.

Down

1. The security guard works at the _____ .

3. She wants to open a checking _____ .

4. Go to the drive-_____ window.

5. Add and subtract in the check _____ .

7. Ten cents is a _____ .

8. One cent is a _____ .

9. One _____ is 100 pennies.

14. The word for 2 is _____ .

Unit 10

EMPLOYMENT

Picture It

The following pictures show people and things that will be discussed in this unit. Refer to these pictures when doing exercises throughout the unit.

1._____ 4._____ 7._____

2._____ 5._____

3._____ 6._____

1._____   2._____   3._____

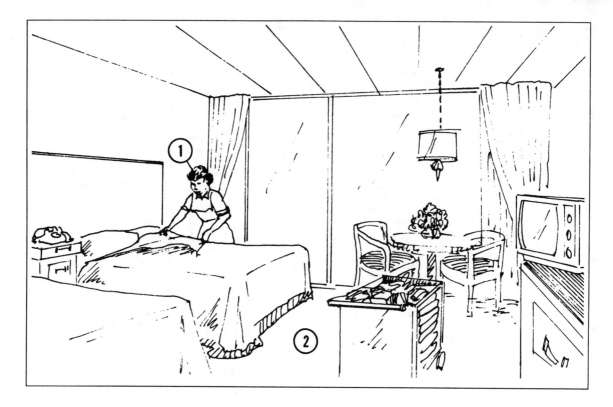

1._____ 2._____

1._____ 3._____

2._____ 4._____

1._____

2._____

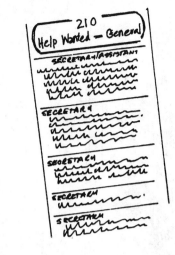

3. _____

4. _____

5. _____

6. _____

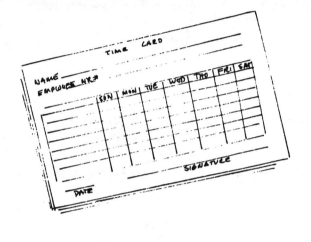

7. _____

8. _____

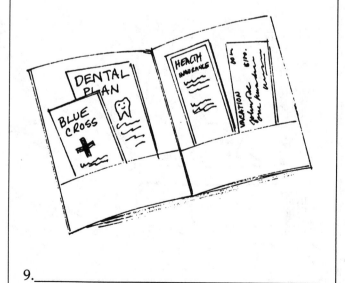

9. _____

Give It a Try

Follow the teacher's instructions to practice the phrases below.

1. The _waitress_ works part time at the restaurant.
   waiter
   cook
   hostess

2. The _housekeeper_ cleans after 2:00 P.M.
   custodian
   busboy
   groundskeeper

3. If you have a question, ask the _receptionist_.
   clerk
   manager
   bellhop

4. The manager tells about the _benefits_.
   wages
   time card
   job application

5. The _taxi driver_ meets the guests.
   bellhop
   receptionist

6. The _secretary_ answers the phone.
   operator
   receptionist

7. Do you want _full-time work_?
   part-time work
   an interview
   a job application

8. I need to ask about _benefits_.
   wages
   paychecks
   the want ad

Attention, Please!

Listen to the teacher's cue. Then, circle the correct response.

1. hostess   desk clerk   groundskeeper

2. cashier   custodian   operator

3. taxi driver   housekeeper   groundskeeper

4. desk clerk   security guard   waitress

5. bellhop   waiter   cook

6. secretary   hostess   housekeeper

7. taxi driver   custodian   cook

8. waiter   groundskeeper   manager

9. custodian   taxi driver   waitress

10. receptionist   groundskeeper   desk clerk

11. busboy   security guard   secretary

12. secretary   custodian   groundskeeper

Tell Me About It (Part A)

Study the picture. Then, ask your partner the questions below. Using your partner's answers, write each underlined name in the correct place on the picture.

Where is the <u>groundskeeper</u>?   Where is the <u>bellhop</u>?

Where is the <u>housekeeper</u>?   Where is the <u>receptionist</u>?

Where is the <u>hostess</u>?   Where is the <u>cashier</u>?

Where is the <u>waitress</u>?   Where is the <u>secretary</u>?

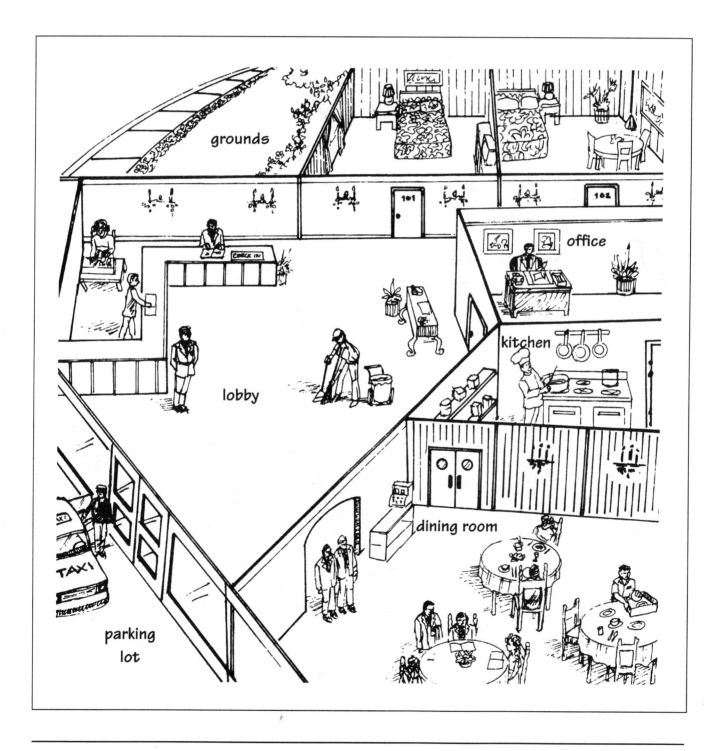

Tell Me About It (Part B)

Study the picture. Then, ask your partner the questions below. Using your partner's answers, write the name of each underlined item in the correct place on the picture.

Where is the <u>cook</u>?

Where is the <u>busboy</u>?

Where is the <u>security guard</u>?

Where is the <u>desk clerk</u>?

Where is the <u>manager</u>?

Where is the <u>custodian</u>?

Where is the <u>operator</u>?

Where is the <u>taxi driver</u>?

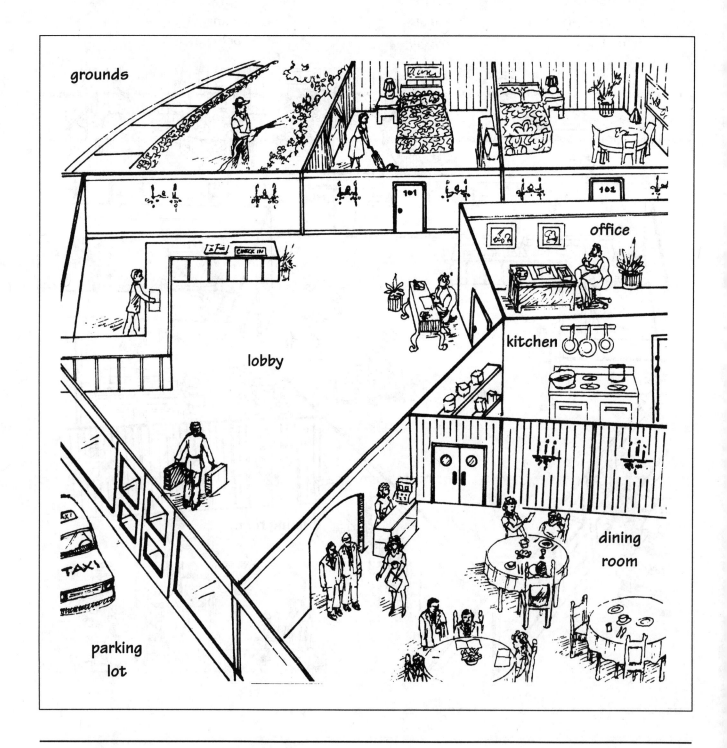

Guess Who, Where, or What

Read each word or phrase in the list below. Ask a classmate if the word or phrase describes a person, place, or thing. Write the words in the correct category.

desk clerk   receptionist   job application
wages   custodian   cashier
benefits   lobby   kitchen
restaurant   housekeeper   groundskeeper
job interview   cook   guest rooms
personnel office   hostess   manager
time card   grounds   bellhop

Workers in a Hotel	Places in a Hotel	Things to Ask About a Job

Two Against One

Circle the word that doesn't belong to the set. Explain your choice.

1. lobby   bellhop   desk clerk

2. part-time   time card   full-time

3. waitress   groundskeeper   taxi driver

4. custodian   housekeeper   manager

5. cook   operator   busboy

6. bellhop   restaurant   personnel office

7. grounds   custodian   groundskeeper

8. paycheck   wages   job application

9. security guard   secretary   receptionist

10. restaurant   desk clerk   hostess

11. receptionist   baggage   telephone

12. taxi   keys   desk clerk

Inside Story

Read the story below. Choose words or phrases from the list that have the same meanings as the words or phrases under the lines. Write the correct words on the blanks. Read the story again using the words written on the blanks.

part-time	work	paycheck
tired	bellhop	security guard
luggage	afternoon	groundskeeper
cook	time card	Sometimes
morning	Friday	

Sokha the Bellhop

Sokha is a _____ at the Madison Hotel. He works
(bag carrier)

_____ . _____ the days seem so long. He
(half time)   (At times)

punches his _____ at 7:30 every _____ and
(time sheet)   (A.M.)

carries _____ , opens doors, and answers questions all day.
(bags)

On Friday he was _____ . His friend Sam, the
(sleepy)

_____ , smiled and gave him a flower. His friend Marcos, the
(gardener)

_____ , gave him some coffee. His friend Sally, the
(night watchman)

_____ , gave him a piece of cake.
(chef)

Sokha felt better at 3:30 that _____ . Someday he will find better
(P.M.)

_____ . But _____ is payday, so he picked up
(employment)   (Fri.)

his _____ and went to his English class.
(wages)

Take Your Pick

There is a missing word or phrase in each sentence below. Read each sentence. Then, look at the three choices under the sentence. Choose the correct word or phrase and write it on the blank.

1. Urick wanted to _____ for a job at the hotel.

   apply   application   applying

2. He had to _____ an application.

   fill in   fill out   fill about

3. The secretary works 40 hours a week. She is a _____ employee.

   fill-time   time-full   full-time

4. Raul has _____ as a security guard.

   experience   experienced   experiencing

5. The custodian _____ from 7:00 A.M. to 3:00 P.M.

   working   works   work

6. The waitress is paid _____ .

   by the hour   by hour   the by hour

7. Erin has an _____ in 30 minutes.

   interviewing   interviewer   interview

8. Raul read the _____ in the Sunday newspaper.

   wanted ads   want ads   ads want

9. Where's the _____ ?

   office personnel   personal office   personnel office

10. There are no _____ with this part-time job.

   benefits   benefiting   beneficial

Bingo

1. Make your bingo card.
Your teacher reads a word or phrase. Choose any square and write the word or phrase inside that square. Write one word or phrase in each square. Don't fill in the squares in order.

2. Check your spelling.
The teacher writes the words on the board. Find the correct spelling of each word and check your card. Correct any mistakes.

3. Play bingo.
The teacher reads a clue. Find the square containing the word or phrase that has the same meaning as the teacher's clue. Cover the square with a marker. When you have three covered squares in a row, you have BINGO!

Get It Together

There is a word missing in each sentence below. Choose the correct word from the word list. Print that word in the boxes of the puzzle.

bellhop   taxi   housekeeper   groundskeeper
ads   check   waiter   pay
clerk   full   security   time
hostess

Across

4. The _____ cleans guest rooms.

6. Look in the want _____ for a job.

8. The desk _____ gives the guest a key to his room.

10. The _____ driver stopped in front of the hotel.

11. The _____ carries your luggage.

Down

1. The _____ plants flowers.

2. Fill out a _____ card.

3. The _____ guard watches over the hotel.

4. The _____ seats people in the restaurant.

5. Pick up your _____ check on Friday.

7. The _____ serves food in the restaurant.

8. Cash your pay _____ .

9. I am looking for _____-time work.